# MARION JONES
## *LIFE IN THE FAST LANE*

# MARION JONES

## LIFE IN THE FAST LANE

An Illustrated Autobiography by Marion Jones with Kate Sekules

Produced by Melcher Media

WARNER BOOKS

MELCHER MEDIA

NEW YORK   BOSTON

This book was produced by Melcher Media, Inc.,
124 West 13th Street, New York, NY 10011.
www.melcher.com

Publisher: Charles Melcher
Publishing Manager: Bonnie Eldon
Editor in Chief: Duncan Bock

Project Editor: John Meils
Editorial Assistant: Lindsey Stanberry
Production Director: Andrea Hirsh
Photo Research: Alice Albert

Art Direction: Joshua Berger
Design: Joshua Berger and Todd Houlette
www.joshuaberger.com

Warner Books

Time Warner Book Group
1271 Avenue of the Americas
New York, NY 10020
Visit our Web site at www.twbookmark.com

Printed in the United States of America
First Printing: May 2004

10 9 8 7 6 5 4 3 2 1

ISBN: 0-446-52455-7

Library of Congress Control Number: 2004103431

# CONTENTS

**1.**

DREAM
REALIZED

It's September 23, 2000. An early spring evening in Sydney and the biggest day of my life so far: the Olympic 100m final. I walk out of the tunnel into a Stadium Australia so vast and crammed it's like a second city within the city. I hear people screaming "Go U-S-A!" I mean everywhere, and there are countless flags, and a million flashbulbs are popping so the stands look like a mammoth diamond necklace. I'm with the other competitors making our way across the backstretch of the track and around the curve. We start jogging a little bit and running out of line, and the officials are going crazy at us for breaking from the pack, but there's really nothing they can do at this point. There's nothing any of us can do but run. This is it, finally. I get in my lane, middle lane five, my favorite, set my blocks and do a couple of pop-outs, as normal. As if this is anywhere near normal. The officials tell us it's time to strip down, so I remove my tights and t-shirt and take position behind my blocks, bouncing, focused—except for the huge moths I'm constantly batting out of my face. They seem to be attracted to the stadium floodlights like small kamikaze track fans.

As I'm in my lane, shaking out, looking around, somehow one voice detaches itself from the hundreds yelling "Hey, Marion!" and I recognize the voice. It's the U.S. Olympic point guard Dawn Staley yelling and waving at me like crazy. As a former player myself, I'm a big women's basketball fan, and I just saw the U.S. team win the other day. Now it seems Dawn is returning the favor. I always smile if I see someone I know in the crowd, and I beam a big grin to Dawn, then I laugh because it strikes me: Here I am at the 100m Olympic final, and I'm smiling like it's nothing. I love it. It brings the whole thing down to earth. Maybe it's not such a momentous experience.

I look over to my right and I'm happy to see another familiar face, my training partner Chandra Sturrup, from the Bahamas. We just look at each other and we say: Okay, let's do it now. In a few seconds, she'll be my competitor and it'll be every woman for herself. Some people believe I go around thinking I know I'm going to win, but that's not how it is at all. I'm thinking the opposite, in a way, how this day above all others, these athletes want it to be their turn; they are going to do everything in their power to beat me. It's a little bit me against the world, especially after all the press I've been getting lately, casting doubt on my ambitions. In front of reporters I'm very polite, but as soon as I get by myself in my room, it's *grrrr.* They think I can't do it? Just watch and see. It's nothing specific, just everything is in my system brewing, simmering in my stomach and in my head, giving me that added bit of oomph. And I've never needed that extra push more than now. When the starter says, "Take your marks," I know that this is it, this is really, really it. . . .

◄ The bib I wore while winning my first Olympic gold medal, a treasured and hard-fought keepsake.

In fact, I've already run three times on this track, but it felt nothing like this. Earlier this evening was the semifinal, and yesterday—the start of track and field at these Olympics—we had the first two rounds of the 100m, which are really for eliminating the athletes who run 13 seconds. Track and field is the part of the Olympics everybody waits for, but I wasn't expecting a huge turnout yesterday for those early heats. Even in world championships, big crowds don't come until the last two races—the semifinal and the final itself—and, in the U.S., we barely get a packed crowd for the finals. I didn't think the Australians would be so into it. But when I got my first glimpse of the 110,000-seat Stadium Australia yesterday morning, there, sticking right out the top, I could see the backs of people's heads and their hands waving. They were shoehorned in, stacked all the way up to the top. That's when I thought: Oh, my gosh. It's the real deal. This is really, really happening. My heart started to race. This was what I'd been waiting for all my life. When I was eight years old, I wrote on my chalkboard: *I want to be an Olympic champion*. And I was finally getting to make it a reality.

Now, I'm not going to say it gets monotonous, but I knew I was going to win yesterday's heats. It would have been the biggest surprise of the Games if I hadn't! Especially after the declaration I made a while back that, let's just say, has proven controversial. . . . It was a whole two years ago when I mentioned that I wanted to win five golds in this Olympics. It was only a casual conversation about my future plans; I didn't think it was going to be such a huge deal when I said it. I was young and really excited with where I was in my sport—even in '98, I was number one in the world. (And by the way, if I was a quarterback who said he wanted to try to throw for 400 yards and five touchdowns, I'd just be considered confident.) But suddenly people were saying: That's so cocky! How dare she! By the time I got to Sydney, I'd been on what felt like every cover of every magazine with headlines like "The Quest for Five. Can She Do It?" "Will Marion Jones Fail?" Much like those moths, the press is really in my face. More than ever, I just wanted to get to the finals. I wanted to get on the track and do what I love most, which is not necessarily talking to reporters.

Evening races are always agony for me because of the waiting. The nervous excitement, the anticipation, the butterflies are excruciating, but then again I love it, I *really* love it. It's not fun exactly, but it's special, like standing at the edge of a mile-high cliff staring at the most beautiful ocean—uncomfortable, sure, but also the best place on earth. Of course, this time, my nerves are off the scale. All of today and last night, I felt like I was dancing on hot coals, I was so anxious to get to the final. Even worse, I wasn't able to focus all my attention on the main event, because I still had to get through the semifinal. I didn't get very much sleep last night; I was too busy checking the clock every five minutes. My husband, C.J. Hunter—he was my right hand, a huge support—was nervous for me too, so I don't think he was resting soundly either.

We aren't staying in the Olympic Village but in an apartment I rented 20 minutes from the stadium at Homebush Bay. We spent the evening before watching *Braveheart* on DVD and eating spaghetti with garlic bread that C.J. cooked (okay, and ice cream and cookies—I have a wicked sweet tooth), and I got a massage. I got up around 8 a.m. and sorted out my things. My only small superstition is I have to lay out my clothes in a certain way on the morning of a race (in order, with the outermost garments underneath, all the way to my underwear on top), just to make sure. It's not that I think I'm going to run badly if I don't do it; it's so I don't forget anything and lose focus. I'm a details person. I have to know everything that's going on around me, down to the last dot on the *i*. I like things done a certain way. Anyway, all the rest of that day C.J. and I watched movies and TV, read the paper, read books, checked e-mail—just found things to do until an hour before I had to leave. Then I did my ritual: I ran a bath, good and hot, with some nice scented bubbles, and I just closed the door, closed my eyes and sat there, starting to get mentally ready.

The semifinal race is at 6:30 p.m., and it isn't like yesterday's heats, when I ran hard for only 30, then 50, meters and shut it down; a semifinal is run just like a final. You're vying for lanes—the middle ones are prized and they go to the fastest—and you also want to get a good time to send a message to the others: *Look at this! You'd better be ready for me in the final.* It's a big deal, all right, but it's still not *it*. Believe it or not, I just wanted to get that one over, too.

I always get to the track about two and a half hours before a race. Here, there's a separate warm-up track next to the stadium, but I don't start warming up immediately. I sit down, check out my surroundings, get comfortable, take a deep breath, drink some water; just 10 minutes doing nothing, starting to focus, getting into the zone. Then I'm on my feet, and my coach, Trevor Graham, starts directing my warm-up. I do some jogging, some stretching, some drills, making small last-minute adjustments. After a while, Trevor looks at me and says, "Are you ready to sprint?" I examine the state of me, and no, I am not. I have a little stinger on the side of my right calf. It's a mental thing, probably; nothing's really wrong with my body, but I hop on the massage table anyway, and my guy works on my leg and gets the cramp out, gets me loose. This is the usual routine—we're doing nothing different, nothing special. Then Trevor asks me again: "Are you ready to sprint?" This time I'm ready. I put on my spikes and a voice comes over the speaker:

*First call, women's hundred meters.*

It's time for the semifinals. "Okay," says Trevor, "just do some run-throughs to get used to the spikes on your feet. What do you want to do?" Three years ago, in the beginning, Trevor would have to walk me through warm-ups, but I've long ago learned to read my body and I know what it needs.

"Sprint hard. Thirty meters," I say. And so I take off, once, twice, three times, working on my head angle, my body angle—the little things that mean everything. I'm feeling fine. "Okay, Trevor," I say. "I think one more and that's enough."

▶ *Being on the cover of* Time *magazine leading up to the 2000 Olympics felt surreal to me— and was a totally unexpected honor.*

I've done my last warm-up sprint, my running shoes are on, and I've done my inventory: Is my uniform okay? Is everything in my bag? Spikes, stretching rope, water? Are the right numbers on my chest and my back? (I wasn't kidding about the details). Then comes the final call. It's time to make my way from the warm-up track to the check-in area. I shake hands with Trevor—it's what we've done the whole three years we've been working together when it's time to part. We're not into the hugging thing. This is the last time I'll see him until after the race. Once you enter the room where they mark your name, you can't come back out. The only people in there are competitors and the judges who'll take us into the final call room, where we do our last stretches.

The Olympic Games follow the same routine as most meets, only the intensity is off the meter now. There's not a whole lot of conversation in the call room, and we have a good 40 minutes yet to wait, so it's a challenge to stay loose and focused. Everyone is vying for stretching room, and I have to improvise a jogging path. Another challenge is the bathroom. I always have to go before a race, and, this being the Olympics, I have to find an official to accompany me. (Thankfully, they stop outside the stall, which is not the case with drug tests.) At least I don't have the hassle of a full bodysuit today. The weather is windy but comfortable, and under my sweats and tights, I'm wearing long shorts. I have a problem with the usual female running bottoms—what we refer to as "booty shorts." I was a tomboy growing up anyway, so I'd never have worn those things, but who wants to run in panties in front of thousands and thousands of people? No way. That would never happen. I always see women before the race, right when they should be focusing, busy fixing, pulling, making sure everything's covered. I always thought, Hey, if booty shorts helped you run faster, the guys would be wearing them.

While we're stretching, they're doing the final roll call and then they ask, *Is everybody ready?* We arrange ourselves in our lane order and start toward the stadium track. One last ritual is the bag search. Like everyone, I am assigned my own official who stands right in front of me like the customs man at the airport and checks for electronic equipment—I can't have a phone to call Trevor from the track, for instance. Then I have to show him my uniform to check that my numbers aren't folded or bent, and that any logos conform to a certain size. Then he measures my spikes, because longer spikes that tear up the track would give me an advantage. And we're off.

Truthfully, I don't remember a whole lot about my 100m semifinal. Trevor wanted me to keep something back for the final, so I eased up after the start for a time of 11.01. I was all eyes on the prize in the semifinal; I just did my job.

After the race, a carrier person brings my clothes over and I dress again, but getting back to the warm-up track means battling through the entire world's sports media. They all want a quote: "So, Marion, one word about how you feel about the final. . . ." "Marion, just give us one word . . ." even though I'd asked them not to ask until *after* the race. So I walk by, saying, "Talk to you guys after the final, Talk to you guys after the final. . . ." Eventually I reach the track, find Trevor and hop on the massage table. I just lie there, calming myself down. Trevor's quietly putting things in my ear: "Okay, take a deep breath; let's talk about the final. Just keep an eye on your body position. Make sure you don't pop up out of the blocks too soon. . . ." Little things like that. And then I jog a bit, shake out for a while, do some casual sprints. And now the whole call room routine starts again.

It feels different this time, entirely different. Leaving my coach on the track is something I've never thought about before, but now I look at Trevor and I can see in his eyes that this next moment, this next race, will make or break my career. I don't know what he sees in me: intensity, yes; focus, sure. But something else, too, I think, a little-girl feeling: Am I ready? Because as many races as I've run and as confident as I may be that I'm the fastest runner out there, I've never done *this*. I've never been in a 100m Olympic final with the whole world watching.

There's a small gate on the warm-up track, and once I'm through it, with him on the other side, there's no looking back. Whoa. Is Trevor concerned—or am I—that I'm going to mess up out there? No. But any athlete who tells you they had no doubt before their first Olympic final is definitely lying.

The call room atmosphere is completely charged now. Yesterday in here, I caught some of the really young athletes kind of eyeing me, even imitating whatever stretch I was doing. They're not doing *that* today. These athletes only want to beat me. I've run against all seven of them before and I know their tendencies, even what they do while they stretch. Male athletes try to intimidate each other by talking trash and being confrontational in the warm-up area, but women play mostly non-verbal mind games. Some take up more room than they need, or accidentally-on-purpose knock your elbow, or casually bump into you. For instance, Zhanna Pintusevich-Block always emits a series of bizarre noises, this *whoo-whoo* pumping-up thing that I guess is meant to throw your focus. She's doing it now. I keep myself to myself. I don't get in anybody's way.

What feels like a week or two passes in here. I'm not thinking anything in words, but my whole body and mind are buzzing—to say I can't wait is the understatement of the century. If anyone bumped into me, I'd probably give them an electric shock. But the time finally arrives when the officials come and get us, check our bags and march us out through the tunnel to the stadium gate. I keep reminding myself: Marion, remember this, remember this moment, as we enter the stadium and, oh, my God. It's insane out here. I thought the semifinal was so packed you couldn't fit in another soul, but now it looks as if the massive crowd has cloned itself; I've never seen anything like this. And there's this unbelievable warmth coming off of them, thanks to the Australians. All along, the home crowd has been embracing everyone from Lithuania to the U.S. as if we were all their own. Which is not usually the case in a world championship. I can't stop to stare because I have to follow in line with the other athletes, but I take a mental snapshot. This is, without a doubt, the best feeling that I've ever experienced in my life.

So, for the fourth time in two days, I round the curve to the start of the hundred, set my blocks and test them, take off my sweats and stow them in my crate, shake out, and line up, slapping away the moths. "Take your marks!" I get into my crouch. And, yes, yes, yes, this *is* it. . . .

Except for the false start. Ekaterini Thanou, the Greek sprinter, goes slightly before the gun and we have to return to the blocks and begin again. I get back in line and wait for the signal.

"Take your marks!" I get in my crouch, hands on the track.

"Set!"

I lift my head. I'm ready, I'm ready, I'm ready.

*BANG!*

There's a sprinter from Jamaica, Tanya Lawrence, to the left of me. She's had a great start, and she's even with me until about 30 meters. But then I feel myself separating from everybody else in the field. I pull away, but I don't think I'm so very far ahead, not even when the sound of everyone's spikes hitting the ground fades until all I can hear is my own spikes, a sort of whispery pattering *shloop-shloop-shloop*. No crowd, no breathing. Then, about three strides from the finish line, I realize it. I'm not working for the gold medal I've wanted forever anymore. It's mine. I've won.

I've had lots of time to wonder—my whole life!—how I'd celebrate when I won a gold medal. Being a tomboy, I think I can always control my emotions. I'd always say to myself, "Okay, Marion, you're not going to break down like all those other athletes do. No tears." But the split second it dawns on me that I've won, I'm lost, I'm bawling like a baby. Partly this is because a few steps after the finish, I fling my arms into the air, head over heels in joy and excitement, and I look up into the crowd and somehow, magically, my sight is drawn instantly to the section where my whole family is sitting. I had no idea where they'd be sitting, but there they all are. Not just my brother, Albert, who I knew would sneak down to the rail to high-five me, but all of them: my mother, my uncle from Belize and my cousins. So I rush over, tears streaming, I guess, but there's this barrier—like a moat, though no water or crocodiles—and I can't get to them. So I grab their hands and my mom manages to hug me and she's crying and I'm crying, and I look up above them, where the big screen happens to be, and they're replaying the race. I just can't believe how it looks, how far ahead of the pack I was. It didn't feel anything like that.

# "TAKE YOUR MARKS!"
## I GET IN MY CROUCH.

Someone tosses me a Stars and Stripes, and I also grab my uncle's Belizean flag and take off around the stadium for my victory lap. When I got to the press conference, there were a lot of questions about that flag thing: "We didn't know you were planning this. Were you making a point?" and so on. But to me, it's just my life. My mom is Belizean; I'm half Belizean. That's where my family lives. My father's American. I was born in the U.S. and I love America, but my life is influenced by both cultures. I wasn't out to make any bold statement. Soon enough, I'll be asked to make plenty of bold statements when C.J. is accused of using banned steroids, but for now, my victory lap is untainted. It's a perfect, perfect time.

I don't know how I got to the medal ceremony. I remember standing behind the podium and climbing up, and then the medal's put around my neck. I spend ages gazing at it, picking it up, trying to realize that it's in my hand, around my neck, looking at the back of it, looking at it upside down. I've never seen one before, let alone held or worn one. It's heavy, and the gold is very yellow. Then the flags are raised and the national anthem plays. There's a screen next to the flag, so I'm also staring right at myself looking at the flag, in gigantic movie-theater close-up. And I don't like my expression so I pull a different face for the screen, and I catch the other two medalists at it as well. And I tell myself, no. No more screen. *Look away from the screen.* Watch the flag. And then the flag kind of envelops me and I tear up a little, and I'm also so incredibly happy that I can't stop smiling. All I'm thinking is, This is the best. This is the best it has ever been.

Now, four years have passed and I'm facing the next big challenge of my career, an even bigger one than my first Olympics, in a way. As I write, I'm standing on the brink of—I hope—realizing my greatest ambitions yet. Much has changed. I'm divorced from C.J. I have a son with Tim Montgomery, the men's 100m world record holder. I missed an entire year of competition due to pregnancy and childbirth. I feel stronger and faster than ever. This time I learned from my naïveté before Sydney, and I told the press nothing about what I want to do in Athens. I'll state it here though: My goal is to win nothing but gold. I have a special place in my heart for Athens, since that's where I won my first World Championship in 1997, and it would mean everything to me to achieve my goal in that city. I would like this to be as exciting an experience for me as Athens was the first time, and the only way to achieve that is to win more golds. I don't know if it'll be five events or four, but this time I'm going to eliminate any bronze. I will only settle for gold.

No, let me correct that. I don't care about the gold medals. I have three already and, maybe this is strange, but I'm not always sure where I put them. In fact, even if they were lost or stolen, well, I'd be pretty upset, but I'd get over it. You see, it's not about the hardware. Until you get it, that's what you think you want. But after I won that first gold in Sydney, I realized what I'd really wanted all along was a gold medal moment that I could always have.

Nobody can take away that moment from me. Now all I want is a few more.

NOBODY CAN TAKE THAT MOMENT FROM ME.
NOW ALL I WANT IS A FEW MORE

2.CHI

PALMD
LITTLE
MET
1984   MI

I'd love to tell you about the first time I laced up a pair of spikes when I was four years old, but it didn't happen. In fact, most of my earliest memories from L.A. are somewhat sketchy. I was born in L.A. on October 12, 1975. Home then was a ranch-style three-bedroom house in a nice lower-middle-class neighborhood on the outskirts of Beverly Hills with a big front yard and a detached garage. I remember the garage in particular because of the time we came home to find that my rabbit, who lived in a hutch out there, had been eaten by our dog. There was fur and blood everywhere. I don't know why the memory strikes me as funny now because I was traumatized at the time.

It was my mom and my brother, Albert, who comforted me. I don't recall my dad being there when it happened. My biological father, George Jones, was only married to my mom for six years. By the time I was three or four years old, he was out of the picture—or, at least he wasn't living with us anymore. I continued to see him regularly for some years after he and my mom divorced. I can't say that I'm mad at my father—contrary to what some journalists have suggested. I'm just sad. Or maybe I'm a bit of both. It's confusing.

My memories of him actually living with us are few, but I can remember him being there during one other dramatic homecoming—when we got back to find that our house had been burglarized. I can recall the feeling of dread I had to this day. Mom went through the place with my father to see what was gone; I'm not sure what they found missing—the TV and VCR probably—except for my father's Certs. He was really upset that his breath mints had been stolen. I don't mean to make him sound weird or angry, because I don't remember him like that. He was strong-willed, independent, and to me, a four-year-old daddy's girl, he was wonderful. I think the great Certs robbery just perplexed him.

In truth, it was my brother, Albert, who was my great and lasting hero. Albert Kelly is my brother from my mom's first marriage, and he's five years older than me. I looked up to him. I followed him around. I wanted to play all the games he was playing with his friends. The games were many and constant, and he was the boss of them; in fact, Albert was the leader of the neighborhood kids in every way. Albert didn't get me interested in sports, because I was born interested, but he certainly helped me get good at them. He believed in me. When he'd pick me for his team—not because I was his little sister, but because he thought I'd help them win—those were my proudest moments. Even before the time of dawn-to-dusk T-ball and baseball and soccer and so on, Albert and I had a special bond. We were tight from the start.

Back then, in the late '70s and early '80s, Albert was attending a private military academy in Long Beach, which was mom's way of supplying him with father surrogates, as well as a better education than our local public schools provided. The school was a long way from us, south of L.A., and he'd come home only on weekends. He was a bright young man, but he was always forgetting his bag of clothes, which he was meant to bring home for washing. Or worse, he'd pick up someone else's clothes by mistake. Finally, my mom had it up to you-know-where on one occasion and said, "Okay, that's it! You're gonna walk back to Long Beach and get it!" She was just trying to scare him, but I piped right up: "Mom, if you send Albert away, then I'm—I'm going, too." And I grabbed his hand and marched him out the door. I can still see myself in my little flip-flops, holding my brother's hand, walking, headed to Long Beach. I think Mom let us go several blocks before she fetched us back.

I guess that was an early example of me exercising my independence; it's something I've always done and, later on, it occasionally led to friction between Mom and me. Some people call Mom "Big Marion" and me "Little Marion," and not *just* because we share a name. I definitely take after her in some ways. My mom has always been strong—she had to be. She came to America in 1968 from Belize, and made her own way. She always worked her fingers to the bone for Albert and me, mostly as a legal secretary, but often holding down two or three jobs so that my brother and I could attend private schools and enjoy our sports. She and I are very close, but we do have our differences, and over the years we haven't seen eye to eye on everything. We've never had one of those cozy, giggly relationships where you gossip about boyfriends and such. That's not her and it's not me either. I was a tomboy from the beginning, and willful too. Still, when I was a kid, there was no question that Mom was the boss. There were codes of conduct: We weren't allowed to curse, for instance; in our household, saying "hell" was bad enough—we didn't even know the f-word. Mom was a wonderful teacher when it came to manners; there were no lectures, we simply learned from her example. She was also a disciplinarian, if necessary. When we did wrong, we got a whooping with the belt or the switch. A lot of people don't believe in disciplining kids that way these days, but I know that if I'd gotten a little slap on the hand, it wouldn't have had any effect at all. I'd have gone right back out the next day and done the same thing. Sometimes I did anyway.

Mom's system worked, too, because there were no fights in our house. We simply understood the rules: What Mom says goes. Respect for others was key, which was a major difference between Mom and my biological father—his manners left a lot to be desired. Mom doesn't have a lot of good memories of him. Although she never talked much about him—she thinks it's better not to say anything at all than to be negative—I think she believes he simply wasn't a good man. So when Dad left—and I believe it was my mom who threw him out in the end—I didn't really understand that he wasn't coming home anymore. We just never had that conversation. Divorce is a common topic now, but back then it wasn't mentioned, at least not in our household. He just stopped being around. I still saw him regularly though. He owned a laundromat in L.A., and Mom would drop me off at it, or at his home, about once a month until I was maybe seven years old. He would lavish me with attention and introduce me proudly as his daughter to any friends and family who came around. And I loved seeing him because he spoiled me. If I wanted candy, I got candy. If I wanted soda pop, I got soda pop. If I wanted change in my pocket, I got it. And he always sent me birthday and Christmas cards.

When I was around seven, we moved out of L.A. to Palmdale and I really started getting into sports. It was a further drive to my dad's, so I saw him less. And by this time, my stepfather, Ira Toler, was in the picture. I first met Ira when I was about six years old, and I took to him right away. He was retired from the postal service and before that the military, and he was much older than Mom, though I didn't notice that at the time. Neither did I catch on that he and my mom were dating at first. Mom never dated—she was always cautious about bringing any men around her children. She just introduced Ira to Albert and me, and there he was, which was fine by me because I adored him. He was like a big, wonderful teddy bear you could play with; I would crawl all over him and hang from his neck. And I used to love when we all stayed at his apartment. He had the coolest bed that went up and down by remote control—a hospital-type bed, I realize now, even though he wasn't sick—and I remember that he and I would always go hand in hand to fetch doughnuts early on Saturday mornings.

It was when he and Mom got married that they decided to move us to Palmdale. It was a great neighborhood for kids, and I loved it immediately. Our house was big, with a two-car garage, three bedrooms and a huge garden in back that Ira loved to tend. Since he was retired and Mom now had an hour-and-a-half commute to the Beverly Hills law office where she worked, Ira was a stay-at-home dad. Mom would wake me early, before 6 a.m., and do my hair, then she'd leave for work and I'd go back to sleep. Ira gave me breakfast

▲ *Me and Albert, my brother, at the pool.
He and I would regularly go to the
closest neighborhood public pool to
swim on weekends.*

and got me ready for school. When I got in trouble with Mom, it was Ira I ran to; he was the big softy. When I got home, he was who I saw; if I was sick at school, it was Ira who would come get me, or sometimes he'd turn up and surprise me with a McDonald's lunch. Ira was also a great cook. When Mom cooked, it was occasionally Belizean food (like my favorite shrimp Creole, with tamarinade, or tamarind juice), but Ira cooked Texas-style. He had been a cook in the military and was used to catering for hundreds of men, so when he made dinner, we'd have leftovers for three weeks.

     Palmdale was where I got my first exposure to organized sports. Ira drilled a hole in our driveway for a tetherball pole, and also a basketball goal, and all the kids would come over for contests. Mom and Ira and all the other parents would bring their chairs out on warm evenings and sit chatting while we played. We'd set up baseball games in the street and ride our BMX bikes over the dirt, jumping the hills, and we played everything from soccer to hide-and-go-seek. Then, on Saturday mornings in summer, Albert and I would walk to the community swimming pool, stay all day and stop in at Kmart on the way home for the free water fountains because we never had any money. But I think one of my favorite sports of all back then was T-ball. I *loved* it. If there was a sport that taught me to focus and develop my powers of concentration, T-ball was it. Of course, I learned from Albert. "My big bro, he knows how to play," I told myself. "So I'm going to listen to him, and what he says goes." I remember studying that little ball on the tee and thinking only about the task at hand. "Put all your focus on that ball," Albert said. "Don't let Mom or Ira or even me yelling in the stands distract you. Focus. And put the bat on the ball. . . ."

▲ Mom and my biological father, George Jones, at their wedding ceremony.

▶ The marriage between Mom and my father wasn't meant to be. I recall them together only in my earliest memories.

The first year I played organized T-ball there was another little girl, but when she dropped out, I was the only one. I was faster than all the boys and would always catch up to the runner on base ahead of me. I remember my mom, Ira and Albert yelling, "No, Marion! Stop! Stop!" In the end, Ira and Mom had to take me out of the league because the other teams' parents got out of hand. They'd yell at me too, but not in an encouraging way. They'd shout, "Hit her between the eyes, Johnny! Take her out!" Needless to say, I was upset when I couldn't play anymore.

Most of my memories about Palmdale and sports include Albert because I spent almost all my time hanging around with him and his friends. They did all the rough-and-tumble stuff I loved to do. I keep saying I was a tomboy, but I didn't want to *be* a boy; I just wanted to do the things they did, to be accepted as one of them—and even though I was a girl and five years younger, I was accepted. They'd all want me on their teams. If I didn't get picked, I couldn't stand it; I'd run home crying. So it was the thrill of my life when I was picked at age seven as an all-star in our neighborhood ballot—voted in by Albert's friends, who were five years older, and who were *boys*.

I never really resisted the girly stuff, except for one thing: dresses. I was miserable when my mom dragged me to buy nice clothes, mostly because I had to spend perfectly good outdoor time in some shop, picking out frocks to wear to church or school. We went every Sunday to a Methodist church in Palmdale, and I couldn't wait to get out so I could change back into my play clothes. And the years in Palmdale weren't exclusively about boys' pursuits. I did gymnastics, which I loved, and ballet and tap dancing, which I didn't. Albert would take me to dance practice, which was in the shopping mall around the corner from our house. He'd ride his bike and I'd balance on the handlebars in my tights and my little tutu, with my bag on my shoulder. Once, when I fell off and scratched up my bag and ripped my tights, I had to invent a lie for Mom about what happened because she'd paid good money for that stuff. All I wanted from the dance classes was to progress far enough to get the tap shoes with the higher heel, instead of the little-girl low ones, and get my picture taken. I never did get those heels. Gymnastics was better. I loved jumping and flying and throwing myself around, but unfortunately I kept getting little ankle injuries, and Mom started worrying that the instructors were not properly qualified so she took me out of the classes.

Though most of my early playmates were boys, I did have one really good girlfriend, named Christina. Ira called her Hard Tack. And I was Fast Jack. She was a tomboy, too, so we loved playing together. But not with dolls and mud pies. No, no. We were rough. We'd set up our lemonade stand together and within 10 minutes, the money and the lemonade would be flying and we'd be in a huge argument. The next day, we'd be best friends again. I saw her last year, oddly enough. I was flying home to Raleigh when a flight attendant handed me a note: "You probably won't remember me from your early, early past, but your stepdad used to call me Hard Tack. . . ." The flight attendant turned out to be Christina! And she was just the same. I mean, taller and grown-up and married with kids. But the same Christina. We had a great time reminiscing.

I got progressively more serious about sports as I grew older in Palmdale. Playing with neighbors wasn't enough anymore. I wanted to compete. I wanted be a part of anything sports-related, and my mom was very good at tracking down what was being offered at community centers or any available leagues I could join. When I was seven years old, Ira and Mom heard about an area track meet that took place at my brother's high school in Palmdale. The closest thing I'd seen to a track meet were the semiorganized races we'd have in our street, so I couldn't wait to test myself. I remember the wonderful feeling of that day, arriving with Ira and Mom on a slightly misty morning, the kids all sleepy because it's so early, and me tying on my first numbers in my T-shirt and sweats and my pink high-tops—like Converse All Stars, only a generic brand—that I just loved to wear. There were probably a hundred kids total, and it took place on a dirt track. It's funny, but I don't even remember the outcome. I'm pretty sure I won, but that wasn't the point. What I loved was the newness of it all, the unknown, the anticipation: How does this all work? Which kids am I going to run against? What's going to happen? I felt a terrific sense of mystery. From that day on, I was hooked, though a full year passed before I ran another meet. I competed in the same one the following year, which turned out to be a qualifier for another meet, a bigger one. And so it went on. But getting really serious about running was still a ways ahead.

A defining moment for me happened in 1984, when the Olympics came to L.A. The gold medal winners made an indelible impression on me. Strangely enough, I never put together my running ability and what those elite sprinters were achieving; I didn't see the two things as connected, even though I immediately wanted to be an Olympian. I think that's because I always live entirely in the moment. When I raced then (and now), it was all about who was in the lane next to me and how I was going to beat them. But when I watched the Olympics, I was caught up in another discrete moment, a completely different and particular thrill.

I had my first taste of the Olympic buzz when Ira drove me to the Los Angeles Memorial Coliseum to see the parade for the opening ceremonies. I remember us standing on the side of the road as the athletes went by in cars. I saw the torch and felt this wonderful excitement mounting because the Olympics were going to happen and the best athletes in the world were coming right here. Before that, I'd heard of the Olympics without really understanding what it was. After the parade, I felt a personal connection. I knew I was going to be involved in it one day, somehow.

I'm sure my mom and Albert were there when the events were on TV, but what I remember most about the 1984 Summer Games is sitting on the couch watching them with Ira. He was a big football fan, but he also liked track and field, so we saw all the races. Of course, Carl Lewis and Jackie Joyner-Kersee were competing then, but I don't remember the individual athletes; I just remember the sight of them crossing the line when they'd won. I could see something in their eyes that I had never seen before—a certain glimmer, an intense gleam. I didn't know which part of the experience was shining out of their eyes—the joy of winning a gold medal or the knowledge that they were the best athlete in the world or something else—but I wanted it, and I knew you could only get it by doing what they did. I wanted to feel whatever was causing that expression. I wanted the experience.

A few months before the Olympics came to town, I had another formative experience when Mom, Ira, Albert and I went on a road trip to Belize. Mom hadn't been back in umpteen years so she had mixed emotions, especially about seeing her brother, Godwin Hulse, again after some years. But her worrying was for nothing. The reunion was a total success. For me, the child of a tiny family, it was so fantastic meeting my uncle and my cousins that I immediately fell in love with them and their country. I was in total awe of my Uncle Godwin from the start. His presence was so commanding, his stature upright and proud. He seemed serious and stern—he was highly educated, partly in Germany and England—but also kind and dependable, and he gradually became a definite father figure to me, and a chaperone at many key events in my life. He was—and is—a man of many talents. Not only did he build his own house from walls to wiring (he's a qualified engineer), he also ran an agricultural business, did cattle ranching and rice growing, and he was the president of the Belizean Chamber of Commerce and Industry.

◀ T-ball always put a big smile on my face,
especially as a six year old.

▶ As a youngster, I could never find enough
sports. Soccer was yet another one that I loved
to play.

# I GOT PROGRESSIVELY MORE SERIOUS ABOUT SPORTS AS I GREW OLDER IN PALMDALE. PLAYING WITH NEIGHBORS WASN'T ENOUGH ANYMORE. I WANTED TO COMPETE.

1985

Hi my name is Marion Jones. I'm 5 feet 2 inches. I 10 years old and in the sixth grade. I think I have a nice personality. I have a pretty good grades and my weight 85 pounds.

My hobbies are running and gymnastics. I like running because I can beat almost everyone at my school. I like gymnastics because I can do all sort of tricks and I'm very flexible in some ways.

My plans for the future are to be in the 1992 Olympics. I've been training alot, and the boys at my school are good practice. I know if I don't get in the olympics I have to have a backup so I plan to electrical engineer like my uncle.

I felt a strong affinity to the Belizean culture. I loved the smell of the lush vegetation, the trees and the fruits, the sight of bright colored clothes hung on lines, and I loved how all of life was lived outside: little barefoot kids running around, girls braiding each other's hair, women holding their babies chatting in the street. I could hardly blame my mother when later, she sent Albert to Belize to live with his uncle. She felt the public school system in California was letting him down, and that the military academy had failed to fill that father-shaped gap in his life.

Albert had been living in Belize for three years when Ira started having headaches. The headaches got worse and worse until Mom had to stay home from work to look after him. She had to close all the shades because he couldn't stand the sunlight. Then he had to start sleeping on the couch because it hurt just to get up and move around. He went to a doctor, who told him it was nothing, "probably high blood pressure."

One morning, as I left for school and kissed Ira goodbye as usual, I felt something wasn't right. When the phone rang in the classroom two hours into class, I knew it was for me. "Marion, your mom's up front," the teacher said. "She's taking you home." And Mom told me how, when she'd got back from dropping me off at school, Ira had been lying there on the ground where he'd fallen trying to get to the phone. She'd called an ambulance. Ira had had a stroke.

I don't know how long he stayed alive—a day and a half or two. At that time they didn't let minors in to see critically ill patients. I was so upset that my mom promised she'd persuade the nurse to sneak me in, but it never happened. I never saw Ira again.

Because he was such a great, genuine person, it was no surprise that he had tons of friends at his funeral. We were in the front row, of course, and I spent what seemed like forever staring at his nose and the top of his head sticking out of his coffin while people trooped past to view him and cry and pay their respects. I didn't get up because I hated the idea of seeing Ira like that. I decided then and there, I was not going to have an open casket at my funeral. I want to be remembered happy and alive.

After a while, I couldn't stand being there anymore so I asked my uncle to take me to the bathroom. We walked down the aisle with him holding my hand and everybody was looking at me. I knew they were thinking, "Oh, poor little girl. She can't take it," and I hated that they were thinking that. But I didn't cry. I shut down my emotions.

Later, at the wake at our house, I had to get away from them all, so I ran out and down the street and met a neighbor, a little girl who asked me, "What happened down there? Is everything okay?" And I told her Ira had died, and she stared at me and said, "And you're out here playing?" I shrugged. "Yeah," I said.

I acted like Ira's death didn't bother me, just as I'd said it was no big deal that I didn't get to see him one last time at the hospital, but in fact I had no idea how to deal with the pain. Mom was inside, obviously hurting, and being comforted by her brother, back from Belize with Albert. And Ira's family was inside comforting each other. Even my brother was busy comforting my mom. They didn't pay attention to me because I wouldn't let them. But also, even back then, I guess they were thinking, "Don't worry about Marion. She has it under control."

◀ *Even at age 10, I wanted to be a sprinter . . .*
*or an electrical engineer.*

3. ON

TRACK

After Ira's death we left Palmdale and moved to Sherman Oaks so Mom could be closer to work and I could go to a private school called Pinecrest Elementary. According to Mom, I'd been showing signs of rebellion, and she figured the California public school system (which was very poor in the late '80s) was partly to blame. Frankly, it was not the best of times. I was lonely. Albert was back in Belize, and Mom was putting in longer hours than ever to make the expensive tuition for my new school by working for the Beverly Hills lawyers and also taking classes in medical and legal transcribing. And for what? To send me to a school I hated.

Pinecrest was full of hoity-toity "gag-me-with-a-spoon" Valley Girls—and they were all white. I remember only three other students like me. Not that this seemed like such a big deal, but it began to bug me a little that 95 percent of my schoolmates didn't look like me. On the positive side, Pinecrest was where I got my introduction to basketball. Back in Palmdale, I used to mess around shooting hoops, but Pinecrest had a whole program, run by my first real coach, Geoff Jarvis. I quickly made the team after developing rudimentary skills by playing with boys on the courts at recess. There was no track at Pinecrest, but Mom found me a local club, the West Valley Eagles, to give me the experience of running with a team. I started traveling to meets in different cities, then in different states, and soon I was competing in regional and national junior championships. My track career began in earnest.

It's funny, but no individual track coaches from back then stand out in my memory. What I do recall is hanging out with all the other kids in the club and being taught how to stretch—incorrectly. One time, I was pushed into touching my toes so forcefully that I woke up the next day with the back of my thigh black and blue. I'd torn a hamstring. The memory of it makes me think that the lack of expertise in coaching children is a problem, one that still exists. I mean, parents are very kind to give up their time to coach kids, and we do need those volunteers, but there really needs to be some kind of basic training program for local coaches. Technique and safety are crucial. Teaching young kids about motivation and concentration, which is the trend these days, really isn't enough. Sometimes I'm asked if I ever deliberately learned concentration or visualization techniques, but I have to say it's always come naturally to me, to zero in on the task at hand. And my speed? Well, I've been blessed. It has always been there.

It does cross my mind from time to time to whom I owe my supersonic fast-twitch muscle fibers (the kind you need for an anaerobic activity like sprinting). Surely they're at least partly inherited from my biological father. I guess he was on my mom's mind, too, after we moved to Sherman Oaks—but in a different way. I needed travel money and equipment to attend meets all over the place—in addition to the school tuition—and Mom was really struggling. My father hadn't contributed any child support since I was seven or eight (and even then, it was hardly anything), so Mom asked me to get on the phone with him to see if he could help. It wasn't necessarily financial support she was looking for him to contribute, but something practical. The upshot was dad agreed to pick me up from school and take me to stay at his house two days a week.

At first, I was very excited to be more a part of his life. But as our arrangement got under way and we'd drive to his place, picking up dinner en route, I found I didn't feel as close to him as I used to. I'd changed. I understood then how he'd neglected us in the past, and I think he noticed a new, cool attitude in me. Anyway, our arrangement didn't last long; it worked better for me to stay with Mom all week. After I'd stopped my regular visits, my father quit sending birthday cards. And I can't remember him coming to any of my sporting events—ever. Whereas my mom made countless sacrifices so that I could be in sports, my father did virtually nothing—no significant financial help, no moral support. And that hurt.

In 1989, after only a year or so in the Valley (partly because of its geographical unsuitability, but mainly because it was time to start high school) Mom moved us to an apartment in Camarillo right outside of Oxnard, which was where Rio Mesa, my new high school, was located. Things looked up. Albert came back from Belize and lived with us for a while, working at odd jobs, and I loved Rio Mesa. I found my niche. There were lots of people like me there, and plenty of African-American, Mexican, and white kids. I was playing basketball and running track—and the stage was getting bigger.

Until then, I'd been running against other high school kids and had no doubt that I was faster than everybody else. But in my sophomore year at Rio Mesa, I got my first chance to compete against elite runners. I was asked to an annual meet at UCLA called the Jack in the Box Invitational, a very prestigious event (it's still going, but now it's called the San Diego Indoor Games), one they don't normally open to 14-year-old girls. I was flattered by the honor, but also a little blasé about it; that's how I coped with the pressure of running against the world's best athletes, including a big hero of mine, Evelyn Ashford. (I had

# AND MY
## WELL, I'VE BEEN BLESSED
## IT HAS

two pet parakeets when we lived in Camarillo because we didn't have space for dogs. One was named Evelyn; the other was Carl.) Another trick I used to psyche myself up was to imagine what the competitors were thinking about me. "They think you're an upstart," I told myself. "They think you're coming here to try and make them look bad." I knew it wasn't true—I mean, I'd never met these ladies before—but I convinced myself totally that they really were thinking badly of me. Here's a secret: I still use the same mind game. Nowadays it's easier to come up with those scenarios, since I know how certain athletes feel about me. Before a race when I run now, I might be thinking, "They don't like me. I know they're jealous of me. So I'm gonna go out there. I'll show them." I find it excellent motivation. It gives me that extra edge.

# SPEED?

# ALWAYS BEEN THERE.

◀ *Winning the Gatorade National Player of the Year award three years straight (1991–1993) is an accomplishment that still makes me proud.*

▶ *Basketball quickly became a love of mine. Later, it would end up being my ticket to a college athletic scholarship.*

Later, in 1991, I was named National High School Athlete of the Year for the first of three straight years. I also qualified for the USA Track & Field Championships, which were held at Randall's Island, New York. Again I lined up in the blocks with Evelyn Ashford, and with the great Gwen Torrence, too. Again I was happy to find myself cool and collected. "Watch out, Gwen; watch out, Evelyn," I thought. "Here I come." When I placed sixth in the 100m and fourth in the 200m, I knew I'd be running alongside them soon.

Back at school, luckily, I was able to keep these successes separate from my day-to-day life. I've always wanted to be normal, and I was not into bragging. On the track, sure, I was aiming sky high, I was superteenager. I was famous around the California track scene, which is a very intense, small world, and I was also beginning to be known outside the state. But the guy next to me in science lab wouldn't have a clue about all that. He would know I was a jock, but that was it. Meanwhile, I was going through all the usual teenage stuff—pressing my mom about getting my driver's permit (which I didn't get until I was 22!), hitting puberty, getting interested in boys.

Puberty was hard for me at first because of the tomboy thing, because I don't like dressing up, or makeup, or getting my hair all dolled up—and that's exactly what all the girls with boyfriends enjoyed doing. I figured, well, if a guy's not a jock then he probably won't be attracted to me. And I thought guys were a little intimidated by girls who are athletic and outspoken and talk loud and aren't into diets. So I had boy friends, but not boyfriends, and most of my girlfriends were jocks too. But I wasn't completely out of synch. I'd had little crushes back in elementary school in Palmdale—and my first kiss! I remember setting it up, telling a girlfriend to tell his friend to tell *him* to meet me behind the classroom trailer after school. I remember distinctly that he had this cute little cowlick curl. (Now, what on earth was his name?)

My first real boyfriend was Tony Ontiveros. We started dating in my freshman year at Rio Mesa. He played Junior Varsity basketball, and some of his friends used to hang out with some of mine. When the annual Sadie Hawkins dance was coming up, everyone was hooking up to go. So one day after practice, I found Tony outside the weight room and asked him to the dance—not in any kind of mushy way; it was more like teasing, but not even flirtatiously, not at first. Then his mom picked us up one day after school to go to the mall and choose outfits because you had to dress alike for the dance. We picked out matching Chicago Bulls shirts.

We didn't end up going to the dance. We went to play miniature golf instead, though I'd told Mom I was going to the dance with a girlfriend. Mom and I didn't have the type of relationship where I'd confide the "Mom, I think he likes me" stuff with her. We never had those sort of conversations, and that was fine. I let her think Tony and I were just good friends, which was nothing unusual since most of my friends were guys anyway. He'd come over for dinner or I'd go to his place or we'd go out. And Mom liked him—with good reason. He was a nice guy. Tony and I were kind of together the rest of my time at Rio Mesa, right up until my junior year, when I transferred to Thousand Oaks High School.

▲ Me and Tony Ontiveros, my first real boyfriend, in our prom photo.

◀ As a Lady Lancer at Thousand Oaks high school, I was able to really develop my basketball skills. We regularly played the top high school teams in California, which was great preparation for playing at the collegiate level.

The idea behind this third move was to get me into a serious basketball program. I'd been enjoying the basketball at Rio Mesa—I'd score 40 points in a game and it was a lot of fun—but we didn't play the caliber of teams necessary to develop my skills. During my time at Rio Mesa, I'd also been attending a Saturday basketball camp in Pasadena that had a wonderful coach my mom found, Mel Sims. Coach Sims's sole aim in life was to improve the fundamental skills of girls. I went to the camp every weekend for years—so long that I ended up as a camp counselor. And my game improved immeasurably. Coach Sims's near obsession with basketball, along with his support and advice, were incredibly important to me. And when someone let slip that I was a track star, he started attending my meets and was supportive in that area as well. In 1991, when he asked me to be on an all-star team that was traveling to the Far East, I was determined to go. Mom, bless her, took on even more work and somehow raised the $2,600 to send me on the trip to China and Hong Kong, and off I went.

It was my first real trip overseas and it was awesome! I loved seeing a different culture on its own ground, as opposed to the transplanted Chinatowns here in the States. In some villages, the little kids had never seen a black person, so they'd run up to us and rub our skin. But it didn't make me feel odd; it just brought home the vast differences in our ways of life. During one outdoor night game, I remember there were bats flying all around us and I took off running on a break and passed everyone on the court; the crowd went absolutely insane, standing and stamping and cheering for 10 minutes. Later, I found out that Coach Sims told the Chinese commentator that I was a top high school track athlete and it got translated into "fastest runner in the world." I didn't mind that in the least.

Basketball became much more important after Mom and I had decided I should attend college on a basketball scholarship instead of track. I'd started receiving letters from colleges at the beginning of my freshman year (by the end of my senior year I'd gotten more than 400 of them), and the vast majority wanted me for track. I had no intention of choosing between the two sports I loved. I always knew I wanted to do both in college, so I had to get in on the strength of my basketball because I wasn't nationally known in that. If I took a track scholarship, then I'd have had to find an extremely open-minded basketball coach to let me play on a team. But any track coach would be bound to let me run if I was there for basketball. In short, I had to realize my potential in my second sport.

Thousand Oaks was definitely the right move for my future, but it felt like I was back at Pinecrest. Or worse. It was a very elitist school in an upper-class neighborhood. I didn't like the students—they were rich kids, cliquey and smug. And I was the only black girl on the basketball team. It was a good school academically, but I didn't like the faculty. At Rio Mesa, I'd really enjoyed certain teachers because they made learning lively and fun. But at Thousand Oaks I felt like nobody—besides my mom—was that concerned with how I was doing academically. It seemed like the teachers were just going through the motions; they didn't make class exciting at all.

But I loved the basketball program and got exactly what I wanted from it. I learned heaps and heaps from coach Charles Brown and was tested to the limit playing the best teams. Thousand Oaks was very well known in the California basketball world. We were always nationally ranked, so the recruiters would flock to the games against other top teams. I was being seen on court by the right people. The track team was also very good. It was run by a gifted coach named Art Green, who agreed to work with Elliott Mason, a sports psychologist (and Evelyn Ashford's former running partner!), when I arrived at the school. They had me racing against the boys most of the time, and I continued to progress despite only training in track outside the basketball season.

Although my sports life was going well at Thousand Oaks, I was far from happy. I was lonely again. It was just Mom and me at home, and I couldn't find my social niche at school. I was going through that age when everything was changing, including my body. Making matters worse, Mom and I weren't getting along. I was acting up, being rebellious because I was so unhappy. Then, to add injury (literally) to insult, I had an accident in a basketball game halfway through my junior season. To prevent falling flat on my face after a layup, I shot out my right hand and promptly broke two bones in my wrist. I was out of action, and the only joy in life at the time was taken away. I felt completely alienated. Poor Mom—I took it all out on her. We didn't have screaming fights or anything; it was more of a standoff. I was sullen. Mom would ask me how I was doing and regardless of whatever was going on, I'd say, "I'm fine."

The worst moment came shortly after I got home from the emergency room with my wrist in plaster. Mom said if I needed anything in the middle of the night, I should wake her up—our bedrooms were upstairs—but I was too proud and stubborn to ask for help. So I got up in the night and managed to slip on the stairs and slam my freshly broken wrist against the wall. But even then I didn't call Mom. I just sat at the bottom of the staircase, bawling, my world crumbling in front of me. To this day, my memories from Thousand Oaks are painful. Mom and I now manage to share a laugh at my catchphrase from that time—"I'm fine, I'm fine, I'm fine!" Mostly though, I'm still not ready to laugh about those days. I feel awful that I put my mom through all that, when she was working so hard to make everything good. It still leaves a bitter taste in my mouth.

Life improved, of course, once I was back on the track and on the court. The following season—my senior year—I averaged 22.8 points and 14.7 rebounds per game and was named California Interscholastic Foundation Division I Player of the Year. On the track, my junior year culminated in my participation in the 1992 Olympic trials. I did okay, finishing fourth in the 200m and missing a spot on the U.S. squad for the Barcelona Games by only .07 seconds. In the 4x100m relay, I was offered a place on the team as an alternate, but I turned it down without hesitation. There was no chance I'd run in the final, so I would've received a medal as a participant in a qualifying round. (That was assuming the U.S. team placed. They did. They won gold.) But for me, getting a medal that way wasn't an option. I wanted to *earn* my first Olympic medal!

My growing celebrity as a sprinter brought Thousand Oaks a great deal of attention. And I was useful to them on the court, too. (In my two years on the basketball team, we went 60-4 and won the regional title.) In other words, Thousand Oaks used me. But I used them, too. It was mutual: I got the basketball exposure I needed. With Coach Green and Coach Mason behind me, I won the state title in the 100m and 200m for three straight years—so often, in fact, that by my senior year, I was hungry for a new challenge. That's when I decided to try the long jump. Not only were my heroes, Jackie Joyner-Kersee and Carl Lewis, long jumpers, but it was the only other event that made sense for me to do. Pole-vaulting wasn't available for girls back then, and neither the high jump nor the triple jump excited me. I'd tried hurdles and disliked them—and also seen people hit them and get hurt. I wasn't about to run anything above 400 meters, and I didn't want to throw things. So it had to be the long jump.

THOUSAND OAKS
HIGH SCHOOL 1992-1993

▲ The Thousand Oaks track team photo from the
1992–93 season—my last year of high school
competition.

▶ Clowning around between classes at Thousand
Oaks. Despite my reservations about the school,
I made some good friends.

It didn't seem very difficult to me. You run, you jump. I mean, I knew I could jump—by then I could dunk a basketball—and of course I could run. So Coach Green (who, admittedly, was no expert in proper technique) showed me a few things, and I gave it a try at a meet. I jumped clear over the pit and landed on the other side in the grass, a distance of more than 21 feet. I went to the state meet, jumped more than 22 feet and won the title, almost breaking the national high school long jump record. I was hooked. My technique was, in a word, horrible. But, hey, I thought, "It's high school. Everybody has bad technique." I could learn the proper way in college.

I guess that first long jump title created a bit of a stir. People wondered if I surprised myself winning right away like that. Well, it's something about me you may have noticed by now: I don't surprise myself much in terms of sports. I expect myself to do well. I know that no matter what, if I put my mind to something, I'm going to achieve success at it. The challenge for me lies in continually pushing myself harder. True mental toughness goes beyond being able to focus under extreme conditions. It lies in being able to see further than mere competition, to move beyond what everybody says you should be doing, to keep finding motivation and inspiration even when everything's going well and you're winning. I didn't know it then, but after a couple more winning seasons, I was going to need all the mental toughness I could muster— when misfortune struck and I lost both my sports at the same time altogether.

4.

LADY TAR HEELS

By the end of my junior year at Thousand Oaks, I was knee-deep in college solicitations. The excitement of getting them had worn a little thin, but the caliber of colleges had been gradually improving. It was clear I'd be choosing among top Division I universities. But which one? I considered the local options, UCLA and USC, both of which I knew well (I'd been visiting the UCLA campus all my life). But somehow I just didn't see myself going to either of them. Mom, who was planning to move with me, liked California but was beginning to tire of the sky-high cost of living there; she encouraged me to look at different states. I started with the East Coast, where NYU seemed interesting—until I discovered their athletic program wasn't so hot. I was keen on the University of Florida, in Gainesville, for a while. Then I considered LSU, but Mom wasn't impressed by their academics.

I didn't really consider the University of North Carolina until Mom told me a story: When she was a little girl living in Belize and her friends asked her where she wanted to live when she grew up, she'd always tell them North Carolina. She didn't know anything about North Carolina, but it had somehow stuck in her mind that she'd live there one day. Maybe she'd read about it somewhere. Anyway, after she told me that, I started reading about it and soon found myself getting very interested in the university's communications and journalism program, and in its women's basketball program. They weren't nationally ranked at the time— the women's team definitely lacked the mystique of Dean Smith's (and Michael Jordan's) Tar Heels—but that was perfect for me. I wanted to go somewhere I could have an impact. If I went to, say, Stanford or Tennessee, I'd just ride the bench because my skills weren't up to that level. In the end, the only college I visited was the University of North Carolina.

They flew Mom and me out to Chapel Hill, and it was love at first sight. We got a tour of the campus, and I spent time with the basketball team, watching them practice, getting to know some of the players and meeting the coaches. I met the track team, too, and everywhere we went complete strangers would say hello. I had no idea everyone was like that in the South. I thought, "Whoa, these people are so friendly!" I felt at home there. Mom and I discussed it and agreed immediately; this is where we belong. In one week flat, I'd accepted their basketball scholarship.

The decision was easy for me, but the fallout was not. Track and field in California is almost like football in Texas—it's huge. And I was California's prodigy at the time. I had a lot of people hounding me, saying, "What are you doing crossing the country for a university not known for track—or even women's basketball—when we've got the best programs in the country right here at UCLA, USC and Stanford?" They thought I was deserting them forever. But what was I supposed to say? I knew exactly what I was doing. But I was in high school—and nobody takes you seriously in high school, even when you're a standout athlete. It didn't really matter to me what they thought anyway, but there was one person whose opinion I cared about: my father's. I didn't think for a minute he'd be against my decision; I just wanted him to know my plans, and yes, I wanted him to be proud of me for getting the scholarship. So just before leaving California, I went to his laundromat. I knew he was there because I could see his car out back—and the guy who worked for him told me he was there. But he didn't come out. So I kept trying. It was always the same scenario; he would never come to the door. I shrugged it off, but I was hurt and, even more than that, confused. Why would he do that? What reason could he possibly have to avoid me? Nobody could explain it to me. Or maybe Mom could have, but I never told her that I'd gone to see him. I guess I needed something to be my secret.

Then it was time to go. We packed up our stuff in a U-Haul and drove across the country. It took about four days. I'd like to say that Mom and I got over the hump and were like sisters during the journey, but it wasn't like that. I am thankful every day that Mom moved out here, but I was 17 then; I felt she would cramp my style. Once I'd made the decision to move on, I wanted to get out there on my own. I didn't want my mother treading on my tail. In short, I was being a teenager. Whatever she suggested, I did the opposite. I just wanted my freedom. Of course, as soon as I'd enrolled and moved into the dorms, Mom got an apartment nearby and was careful not to interfere. I had as much freedom as I wanted.

I felt happy at UNC from the get-go. It was the exact opposite of Thousand Oaks. I felt like I belonged. Immediately, I hit it off with my roommate, a sophomore named Tonya Cooper—or Coop—who quickly became my best buddy. We went everywhere together. When I met my other teammates, I got close to them fast too. Suddenly, I appreciated my time at Thousand Oaks enormously: First, my unhappiness there made me love this place all the more; second, I was grateful that coach Charles Brown always had an eye to my future. Instead of making me a center, as I would have been in any other program, he made me work on my ballhandling skills. He wanted me to learn how to be a point guard or a two guard, because he knew when I got to the next level, I would no longer be the tallest on the team. By the time I got to Carolina, I was better prepared than I might have been, but my ballhandling still needed a lot of work. It wasn't at all clear what my role on the team was going to be.

I was pretty surprised when head coach Sylvia Hatchell called me into her office after my second day of practice and told me that she saw me as a point guard—the pivotal position and the de facto leader of the team. "Are you sure?" I asked. I wasn't ungrateful or nervous or anything, but my skills were underdeveloped. Compared to the other top point guards in the country, I was a greenhorn. I had my doubts about her sanity. "Have you *seen* me dribble?" I asked. But Coach Hatchell had thought long and hard and she figured you can always teach someone ballhandling, you can teach someone to shoot, but raw, natural speed is hard to come by. And so I really dived into it. Every day before and after practice, I'd work hard on my fundamentals with the assistant coach, Andrew Calder. When the season began, I was starting at point guard for the Lady Tar Heels.

And I loved it. I loved the leadership role, even though I had misgivings at first, being a freshman issuing commands to juniors and seniors. But after a few team practices, I relaxed into it. They could see how composed I was in high-pressure situations, and eventually they found they could look to me when things weren't going so well. I was good at rallying the players, pumping them up and calling time-outs when we needed them. In fact, I thrived on all that. My first season was a dream. There I was, finally playing with an entire team of serious athletes, not a motley collection of high school players, some of whom were only in it for the phys ed credits. We practiced hard, we played hard and we had enormous fun doing it.

▲ I immediately clicked with my North Carolina teammates, whom I was close with both on and off the court.

I FELT HAPPY AT UNC FROM THE GET-GO. IT WAS THE EXACT OPPOSITE OF THOUSAND OAKS.

# I FELT LIKE I BELONGED.

We used to play a little trick to get us an edge. There were four of us who could dunk the ball. I was the shortest of them. I'd been able to dunk a tennis ball, then a volleyball, since I was a freshman in high school, but I had trouble keeping my grip on a basketball. (People sometimes criticize the women's game for its lack of dunking without realizing many women have the ability to leap high enough to dunk; it's our smaller hand size that's often the problem.) Imagine you're playing us, we're all warming up and suddenly the crowd goes wild. You turn round and see four of us dunking the ball again and again and again. What could be more intimidating than that? You wouldn't know that I'd just sprayed a little sticky stuff on my hand just for warm-ups so the ball wouldn't slip.

The previous season, 1992–93, the Lady Tar Heels had been knocked out of the NCAA tournament early, and this had a galvanizing effect on the team I joined. In 1993–94 we only lost twice during the regular season, both times to the Virginia Cavaliers. Then, in the Atlantic Coast Conference final, we beat them 77-60. When we reached the NCAA tournament final in April 1994, we found ourselves up against mighty Louisiana Tech, which was on a 25-game win streak. I got in early foul trouble and spent a good part of the game on the bench, going back in only for the last part of the game. When Louisiana Tech scored with only 15 seconds left to take a two-point lead, it looked like it was going to be 26 straight for them, which didn't surprise anyone since we were the underdogs, the upstart team who'd made it to the final by luck. Then a Tech player grabbed a rebound from our shot and I tied her up, which resulted in a "held ball," our possession, with only 0.7 seconds left.

We called a time-out and went back to the huddle and drew up a play. It was an audacious idea, but the only possible decision: We were going to try to win the game instead of tie it. Since we knew Louisiana was going to jam the middle and it would be very difficult to get even a two-point shot in, it seemed our only option was to take the jumper—an outside jumper. And if we were going to take an outside jumper, we might as well take a long one, a three-point shot. We decided on Charlotte Smith for the shot, which was not the most obvious choice since she'd only made 26 percent of her three-point shots that season—but that was the point. They wouldn't be expecting her to shoot. It was a mighty long shot in every sense, but we had nothing to lose except the championship. So at the whistle, as planned, Tonya Sampson, our leading scorer, drew the defenders toward the basket, leaving Charlotte open. This whole time I was marking a defender at the top of the key, just hovering and hoping, my heart turning somersaults. I watched Stephanie Lawrence make an unbelievable pass right past the three-point line to Charlotte. Then Charlotte squared up and knocked it down. A three-point basket! We'd won! In that split second, the national title was ours!

It was one of the most remarkable moments in basketball I've ever witnessed, let alone had a hand in. I don't remember the crowd at all, though there must have been mayhem. I just remember the unbelievable feeling of the sweetest victory I'd ever experienced and the joy erupting from our little team that could. We were over the moon! We were delirious! It took days for it to sink in that we were the national champs.

As a team, we set school records that season in just about everything: victories, winning percentage, free-throw percentage, assists, steals and blocked shots. I set freshman records with averages of 14.1 points and 3.2 steals per game. As a start to my college basketball career, it couldn't have been better. My mom had attended every game, and every game I would find her in the stands and have a chat with her. Those were the only times I saw her during my freshman year. During the holidays, I went back to California to stay with my brother in Oxnard. Somehow, I'd got it into my head that my father should share in my successes; I still hadn't given up on him. I'd been sending him the odd picture along with the UNC media guide, which had news of the Lady Tar Heels' victories in it. But he'd never acknowledged any of it. Still, I got Albert to take me over to his laundromat once or twice per visit. It was always the same deal: I knew he was there, but evidently he didn't want to see me. I continued trying through my sophomore year, but other events took precedence and I stopped trying to speak to him.

Despite that continuing sadness, my sophomore year started out even better than my first year. For starters, three new players joined the team, and they would soon become—and they remain—among the most important people in my life. Coop and I were still roommates and still inseparable, but with the arrival of Tracy Reid, Jessica Gaspar and Melissa Johnson, we had a tight little clique—a clique within a clique really, because I was also close with everybody else on the team. Tracy was a wild, wild kid, a free spirit, one of those people who always has you cracking up. She couldn't have cared less about discipline or authority—and got in a lot of trouble at times with the coaches and teachers—but she was so athletic and so intense that she'd somehow get away with it. We called her Hard Core—not because of her personality, but because of her taste in rap music. Jessica was another free spirit, but of a different kind. She's only 5'4" and she's white, with dark, dark hair; in front of the coaches she'd do as they said and act responsibly, but underneath she had real fire—she was even wilder than the rest of us. On the court she was a tornado. She could come off the bench and help us turn a game around—she was never intimidated no matter who you were. Then there was Melissa. Right away Melissa really intrigued me. She was 6'5" with a mass of red hair, and she was crazy smart; she could get a 4.0 without ever studying. (In fact, she ended up transferring to Harvard because North Carolina wasn't academically challenging enough for her.) On the court, she wasn't the most natural athlete and had to work harder than some; off the court if I had a question about schoolwork or some problem that was bothering me, I'd turn to her. All five of us would hang out as a group; we'd go to clubs or dances and wouldn't leave until every single one of us was ready. Melissa was part of that, but she was also different from the rest. She had so many other things going on with school and in her life. If I ever needed to get away from my party friends, my crazy girlfriends, and be quiet and thoughtful, I'd go find Melissa. From the start, she was a refuge for me, and (so she tells me) I was for her.

Not only did we form this tight little social group, we also functioned like a single unit on the court. We were all but telepathic, anticipating each other's plays, backing each other up—especially Tracy Reid and me. Tracy went on to become 1998 WNBA Rookie of the Year playing for the Charlotte Sting. By her junior year at UNC, she was already a phenomenal athlete. After a couple of practices, we all felt like we'd been playing together for years. If I'd needed proof that I was meant to put my heart into basketball at the time, I had it. In the 1994–95 season we aced the ACC tournament, but unfortunately we were knocked out of the NCAAs in the March 1995 Western Regional. The regional took place at UCLA, so it was sort of a homecoming for me. I had a whole lot of friends there, as well as my brother and his family. At halftime, on my way to the locker room, I happened to look up into the stands and I could've sworn I caught sight of my father sitting up there. I was stunned. I needed to stay focused on the game, so I just thought, "Great, I'll get to see him afterward." Then we lost to Stanford. I was upset because of it, and I wanted all the more to speak to my dad. But when I came back out to find him, he was gone. Just like all my laundromat visits—and just like those, it really hurt. It would have hurt even more if I'd known that that fleeting glimpse would be the last time I ever saw him. In a way, my teenage rebelliousness served me well. I was not given to brooding about my father's elusiveness, nor about my distant relationship with my mother; I was too busy doing my thing. I was on a high, and nothing was going to rob me of that. Or so I thought.

▲ *On and off the court, my teammates and I were inseparable: in the foreground, from left, are Tracy Reid, me, Chanel Wright and Melissa Johnson.*

The All-American Board
of the
N.C.A.A. Division I
Track and Field Coaches' Association

having appraised the performance of
track and field athletes throughout the United States
herewith selects and recognizes

Marion Jones
Long Jump
NCAA Runner-up
University of North Carolina
as a member of its

1994

All-American Track and Field Team

Approved

*G. G. Salee*
Secretary, Division I Track Coaches' Association

*Frank Gagliano*
President, Division I Track Coaches' Association

▲ *In June 1994, I came in second for the long jump at the NCAA track and field championships in Boise, Idaho. I was pretty happy with the finish, considering how little time I had to train after the basketball season ended.*

Even though basketball was so fulfilling, I hadn't forgotten my first love: track. The deal I'd made with the UNC track coach, Dennis Craddock, was that I'd rest for two weeks after the basketball season, then train with him. That didn't leave very much time for track: The NCAA basketball tournament stretched the season well into spring, so we only had about three weeks until the conference finals in track, then only another three weeks until the NCAA finals. I did fine in the long jump in the NCAA meet my freshman year, even though Coach Craddock hadn't improved my technique as I'd hoped. I still jumped like a little kid, running as fast as I could, then flying through the air with hands and feet flailing, then straightening out my legs and banging my feet down in the pit: *whump!* Still, I managed second place at the NCAAs in Boise, Idaho, posting my all-time best distance of 22'1¾". My sprinting was less notable: I finished sixth in the 200m and didn't make the finals in the 100m. Given my extremely limited training, I was fairly content with these smaller victories, yet something in me still expected my performances to be at the highest level, even if I wasn't training like the elite sprinter I aspired to be.

Again I performed okay my sophomore year in track given the circumstances, but I had plans to improve on that—vastly. Coach Hatchell knew about my love for track, of course, and I'd told her right from the start about my grand plan. I was thinking about redshirting my junior year in basketball and training for track with the idea of making the 1996 Olympic team. In fact, I was more than thinking about it; I was wildly excited about it, but I didn't want her to get the idea I wasn't taking basketball seriously. So after the Lady Tar Heels lost in the 1995 NCAA Western Regional, and after my less-than-stellar performance in that year's NCAA track and field championships, I took off to California to train with my old coach, Elliott Mason, and spent the summer with his family.

Right away I felt my speed building, but I'd barely begun my return to form when I got a call from Coach Hatchell. The U.S. team was going to the World University Games, and the team wanted me at point guard. Would I be interested? What a dilemma. I was seriously training for track, but a place on a U.S. team—even if it wasn't *the* national team—was not something to take lightly. It would look very good on my résumé if I wanted to make the national team in years to come. (It would be another two years before the WNBA and ABL would form, so a professional career wasn't a goal then.) I had to accept. So off I went to Colorado Springs to start practicing with that team. There was never a doubt that it was the right decision. After the World University Games, I'd complete the summer in California with Coach Mason, then continue my intensive track program with Coach Craddock back at UNC in preparation for the Olympic trials.

I was having a great time in Colorado. Then disaster struck. In practice, I was diving for a loose ball at the same time as my teammate Katie Smith, who managed to land on my left foot. I knew it was broken right away. After my freshman year at Rio Mesa, a recurring pain had turned out to be a stress fracture in the fourth metatarsal of my left foot, and I'd spent some weeks that summer in a cast. The injury had healed up no problem, but this felt worse. And sure enough, it turned out to be no simple hairline stress fracture. The X-rays showed a break in the fifth bone in my left foot. I flew home to North Carolina for surgery. The UNC surgeon, Dr. Tim Taft, who was famous for preserving Michael Jordan's knees, performed the surgery. Afterward, my fifth metatarsal was held together by a metal screw.

I was utterly miserable. It was shades of how I felt when I broke my wrist at Thousand Oaks, only now the stakes were higher. Nobody could tell me how long I'd be out of action, but obviously it would affect my chances at making the Olympic team. And I wouldn't be playing basketball anytime soon. Coop and I had moved out of the dorms into our own apartment before the accident. At first it was fun because Coop had a car and she'd drive us to campus and to practices, but when I had a cast and couldn't get around any other way, all the fun went out of it. Even so, I'd go to team practices with her and sit on the bench, watching all my friends play. I had to go—or I'd have lost my mind. What was I going to do? Sit alone in the library? So I watched practices and games and went to rehab and did exercises—swimming, stationary bike riding, stretching, weights—to promote the healing, but still I wasn't doing well. I felt myself slipping into a kind of depression.

One bright spot during those dark weeks was a new friend I made. Coach Craddock had recently hired a shot putter, C.J. Hunter, as an assistant coach. I first ran into C.J. in the weight room, where I was spending a lot of time rehabbing my foot. We started chatting and hit it off. He was a nice guy, I thought. A big, nice guy. We became buddies. That Thanksgiving, in 1995, I was going to Albert's in California. School was already out, and I needed a ride to the airport that evening, but there was almost nobody left on campus. I found C.J. in the track office, and he said he'd take me, so we went over to his place to kill the four hours or so until my flight, and we got along famously. When I came back after the break, we just fell into a habit of chatting more frequently and phoning each other. And that turned into going out occasionally to a movie or to dinner. Then we started going out more often, and before I knew it, we'd developed feelings for each other. It was a gradual, organic thing. I just started to feel closer and closer to him. Also, he was an athlete and, as such, was very sympathetic about my injury. And that really helped me through.

Finally, after about 14 weeks in a cast—joyful day!—I got cleared to start training again as long as I took it a bit easy. By this time, the basketball season had ended (the team went 13-14 that year and didn't make it past the regular season) and I was back on the track working out with Coach Craddock. I hadn't been on my feet long when I was doing some drills on a trampoline with some of the other track athletes and came down a little awkwardly, heard a tiny crack and felt an immediate stab of pain. Nobody realized what had happened because I'd finished my turn and walked over to the side without saying anything. But when I quietly tried to put some weight on my foot, I found I couldn't. My heart fell out and hit the floor; I knew what I'd done. I knew it was broken. I casually told Coach Craddock I was going to see the nurse. As I made that agonizingly slow journey, the tears started falling. What was going on here? What else bad could happen? I didn't understand this curse that was dogging me after things had been going so well. I kept thinking over and over, Why me? Why me? Why me? They took me to hospital, and the X-rays confirmed that I had indeed broken my left foot again—the same bone in the same place, and I'd managed to bend the pin. I had to have surgery again, to have that pin removed and replaced by a bigger pin, have bone marrow from my hip inserted into my foot to encourage the bone to heal, and have another cast fitted.

No pun intended, but that second break really broke me. As I did with the first break, I still went to practice, but nobody cared if I showed up late. I'd celebrate with the team when they won, be sad when they lost, and pat them on the back when they came in and out of the game, but I wasn't out there with them. Nobody was relying on me. It didn't really matter if I was there or not—and that feeling was completely foreign to me. I felt like the real Marion was missing, the one who was bonded to this tight clique. We student athletes tended to keep to ourselves. I didn't have friends who were regular students. Maybe I should have made friends with non-athletes, but it didn't seem possible. It seemed there were jealousy issues—they thought we got perks, and it was assumed that the only reason we were in school at all was our ability to play ball. Well, now, without my ability to play ball, I wasn't sure what to do with myself. There was not much of a black student union, no sorority house. When the team went on road trips, I'd mope around the apartment watching daytime TV or take the bus to campus. And I was poor. I couldn't afford cabs. I couldn't afford to call my

▶ *Most of my basketball teammates were unaware of my "secret" history with—and love of—track.*

# I FELT MYSELF SLIPPING INTO A KIND OF DEPRESSION

brother in California half the time. Mom lived down the street and made it clear she was there to support me, but I wouldn't let her near me. And she didn't insist for fear of overstepping her bounds. I wish now that I'd been able to reach out to her for consolation, but my pride wouldn't let me.

That winter seemed interminable. I hate the cold in the best of times, but that year we had a really bad ice storm. One day, when Coop was away, I remember limping out of the apartment on my crutches and slipping on the thick ice. Instead of clambering to my feet or calling for help, I just sat there, melting ice soaking through my clothes, tears streaming down my face. What was happening to me? The success rate in healing stress fractures is high, but I'd pounded it so hard that the metal had warped, and I'd had marrow transplanted. All the jumping on court and into the pit—with my literally shocking long jump style—might have taken too much of a toll. What if my career was over before it had begun? Even today, I still get a sick feeling in the pit of my stomach when certain smells transport me back to that apartment, or even when I drive around that area.

Of all the people I knew then, C.J. was the most supportive. When I broke my foot the first time, back in the summer, my teammates had known what a blow it was and they'd all been there for me. But somehow this time they seemed less sympathetic—not that I was asking for emotional rescue. Even if I was outwardly calm and collected, and maybe even seemed cheerful, I secretly yearned for a little comforting. C.J. picked up on that. He'd bring food to the hospital so I had something decent to eat. When I was home, he'd visit with me for hours on end. I learned a lot about him. He was raised in Pennsylvania, the only child of a single mom. He remained very resentful toward his father for never being in the picture. C.J. was a big-time football player in high school, where he also competed in throwing events. That led to a shot put and discus scholarship from Penn State. After college, he went straight to the professional track and field circuit, touring throughout Europe. He'd won bronze in the previous year's world championships and was looking forward to doing better in the 1996 Olympics. He was a real student of the throwing sports, studying the mechanics of each while challenging himself to get stronger and stronger—we had that in common. C.J. also told me about Corey and Ahny, the two children he had with his former wife, who were four and six at the time. I had no problem with his kids, or with his being seven years older than me. (Later, I learned that some people were less open-minded.) Our relationship deepened. We kept it quiet at first—even if C.J. wasn't *my* coach, liaisons between athletes and coaches were banned at UNC—but when we got more serious, we didn't want to deal with the secrecy anymore. So C.J. decided to quit. He wasn't a big fan of Coach Craddock anyway, so he left the faculty and got a job coaching at St. Augustine's, a black college in Raleigh. And I left my apartment and moved into C.J.'s house.

I understand now what people were thinking then—a lot of people didn't understand what made our relationship work—but I was still in my rebellious phase. I thought it was none of their business—and that included my mother. But suffering those setbacks, missing both my sports and not knowing what was going to happen to me made my mind-set pretty rigid. It was me against the world. And that's how C.J. was. He was a natural rebel. So even though I found him to be a warm and even nurturing person, he did have an edge to him that was the first thing you'd notice. I was attracted to that. I was like that, too. Later on I changed, and C.J. began to seem a little too spiky too often. But in early 1996, he fit me perfectly.

That spring, C.J. and I got engaged. And as my foot began to mend, we talked excitedly about competing together in Atlanta. But it gradually became obvious there was no way I'd be fit enough to compete, and that was a huge, huge blow. When I turned down the alternate's spot in Barcelona, I'd been counting on 1996 to be my first Olympics. But now I'd have to wait another four years—and that assumed my foot would heal completely. When I'm disappointed, I clam up, and that's what I did. I was comfortable knowing that I had nobody to rely on but myself. I guess it's a self-protection reflex I picked up around the time of Ira's passing, when I was hurting a lot but didn't know how to express it. I believed that if nobody knew the real me, they wouldn't have anything on me; if they acted up, messed up or left, they wouldn't be able to break my bubble—they wouldn't be able to hurt me. This, as it turned out, was not a conducive attitude for making the perfect marriage. I would be more open with C.J. than I was with most of my friends. I thought I had let down my shield enough to make our marriage work, but I hadn't. On the other hand, C.J. was emotionally open with me—about his relationships with his mother, his kids, his non-relationship with his father and so on. (I've learned since that he wasn't quite as open as I thought, but we'll come to that.) People still ask me all the time why C.J. and I broke up. "Was it something he did?" they say. And I say, "No, it's probably a lot about what I *didn't* do."

But it was a while before those cracks started showing. That summer, I met C.J.'s mom for the first time—when we sat together in the stands at the Atlanta Olympics. C.J. was hurt and didn't perform too well, but just being there among the athletes snapped me awake from a year of sleepwalking. I hadn't experienced that track and field buzz in so long, and watching Gwen Torrence and Gail Devers in the women's 100m, I felt ravenous, furious, delirious. . . . It should be me! I could be beating these women! I should be out on that track! Yet all I could do was sit there, pray for the best and hope that my foot would finally heal. I thought about my two sports and realized how intensely I missed running, how I loved that feeling of being all alone in the big stadium, with nobody else to depend on. Like I said before, nothing made me more comfortable than having only myself to rely on.

My senior year academically—but my junior year athletically, thanks to my injuries—I was back on court. Coach Hatchell had reminded me repeatedly that I had a fifth year of eligibility and that she'd love me to play on the team another season. She thought we'd go far. She also had her eye on the newly forming WNBA and ABL for me. But while I was polite and didn't turn her down point blank, I knew that this would be my final year as a Lady Tar Heel. I'd gained about ten pounds—I must have weighed 153 or 154 pounds—and I kept getting little nagging injuries. My ankle was wrapped for most of the season, but I was still aggressive and able to move well on the court and put up good numbers. I was still a team leader, and mentally I was all there, but I wasn't quite myself. Even though I'd been so eager to get back out on court and my teammates had missed me and I felt needed and the team did very well again after the terrible 1995–96 season, it was the track where I really wanted to be. I wanted to compete again, sure, but I was just *aching* for the intense practice sessions I hadn't really had in four years, since high school. I wanted to be out there, all alone, pushing and pushing my body to its limits.

Strange as it may sound, the only one of my teammates who had any idea of my high school career in track and my continuing allegiance to another sport was Melissa Johnson. She was my chief confidante even at the best of times, but now I really leaned on her to help me formulate what I was going to say to the team. I needed them to understand fully why I was leaving at the end of the 1996–97 season, and I needed strategies for how I'd cope if I broke down while I was telling them.

I imagine a male player's parting speech would go something like this: "Hey, guys. I'm outta here." But women are different. Over the years we had gotten so very close—and part of our bond was the unlikelihood of our being able to make a living at this later on. The WNBA (and the short-lived ABL) were about to form, but apart from two or three of the league's top players, a WNBA player still has to work her tail

▲ C.J. was my strongest—and "biggest"—support
during my injuries at UNC. It didn't take too long
before we became more than friends.

off to pay the rent. And as for playing for a Division I school, we got very few benefits compared to the men. We learned quickly that we could only really rely on each other; we played for the sake of playing, for the sheer love of the game and for the love of each other, without a thought to where it might lead and how many millions we might make. At times, our second-string status annoyed us, especially when we watched the men get on a cushy airplane to take them to their games while we boarded a bus. But we got over it because we loved the game so much. Anyway, the upshot of all this was that I was dreading my farewell speech. I'd reached a kind of mother-hen position by then; I truly was the team leader, and I was sure they'd feel deserted.

Standing before these women, my dearest friends, in the locker room, I almost started crying before I said a word, but I managed to spit it out. I said I was going to take up track and field full-time, and told them a bit about my past—how I'd been national high school champion and qualified for the 1992 Olympics, and so on—and what do you know? In no time flat, everyone was crying. There were tears of joy and excitement for me, and for the loss of their team leader and virtual big sister, and for sentiment, seeing their good friend going out into the world to follow her dreams. And as soon as I saw they understood, I realized that *of course* I'd always known they'd understand. And yet part of me wanted them to be a bit more selfish: "How can you leave us now? Why aren't you gonna help us out when we've gotten this far together?" But it was the coaches who had that reaction. The detached professionals took it very badly.

Anyway, the die was cast and I was about to launch myself into another new start. And I couldn't wait. Of course, there was a lot of lingering sadness. Aside from my yearlong sportless nightmare, I'd just had the best times of my life during the three seasons as a Lady Tar Heel. To this day, I absolutely *love* the college game, and although I preferred the ABL—I thought it was a more fundamentally skilled game—I think the WNBA is getting better and better. I would love to see how I'd rank among the best female basketball players in the world. I don't know if, by the time 2008 comes around, I'll have the spunk for it any more or if I'll even want to deal with traveling and being away from home so much. But it is a little personal goal of mine to resume that part of my career someday. Because although I said goodbye to basketball that day in 1997, it didn't feel like I was leaving it forever. It did cross my mind that I might get another chance to play ball.

▶ *Despite the individual milestone of scoring 1,000 points, the thing I loved best about hoops was the team play.*

◀ *Tonya Cooper and me at graduation in 1997. Life was about to change—and I couldn't imagine how fast it would all happen.*

# 5.

# DING UP

If I could do it all over again, I probably
wouldn't play two sports in college. It seemed so simple
at the time—I had played at a high level in both sports at
high school, so why should college be any different? But
it was a lot more difficult than I expected. I was always
juggling 50 things at once—basketball and running, of
course, but also classes, a social life and so many other
things. By spring 1997, things began to settle. My final
basketball season was over, the injury nightmare was
fading into the past, and I knew I was going to graduate.
So I was finally able to focus on one thing: training. I was
back on track—in every sense.

It was easy getting back into running shape.
I was quickly down to 147, 148 pounds. just by working
out on my own, running sprints and lifting weights. The
weight room was C.J.'s domain, and he was often with
me in there, helping out. Weight training for sprinters isn't
just about the lower body. Obviously, we do a lot of
Olympic lifts—power cleans, snatches and squats—to
build our legs for explosiveness out of the blocks, but it's
important to keep everything in balance. So we also work
with dumbbells—doing side-ups, front raises, over the
head, bench presses—plus we do leg presses and
extensions and all kinds of abdominal work. I had the
weight training down, but I wasn't getting any technical or
mechanical coaching on the track. C.J. and I would
simply decide what I'd do on a given day—for instance,
six 200s in a certain time, at a certain pace, plus rests.

Converting my basketball body back into sprinting shape
had been my first priority. But after that was under way,
I needed some specialized training, especially in the long
jump, which C.J. knew nothing about.

I was training at the UNC facility in the
evenings when the track team wasn't there, which got to
be too much, so C.J. suggested we try going over to the
track at North Carolina State in Raleigh where we'd have
more freedom. I was doing starts over there one day
when I realized someone was watching me intently.
I recognized him, since C.J. had pointed him out to me
before as a coach of some repute and experience.
After a while he came over and asked me, "Do you mind
if I correct something?" I let him change the angle of
my head slightly, and to my surprise, I felt an immediate
improvement; I was more explosive out of the blocks.
Over the course of the session, he changed a couple
more tiny things that also had positive effects on my
performance. I was delighted. What I didn't know was
that I'd been set up by C.J. This was a coach-athlete
blind date.

At St. Augustine's, where he was coaching
then, C.J. was friendly with the former world champion
400m sprinter Antonio Pettigrew. At some point I
guess my name came up along with the fact that I was
graduating and looking for a coach. Antonio, who

apparently knew of me from back when, suggested his own coach, Trevor Graham. Trevor had run the 400m and the 400m hurdles for the Jamaican track team and also for St. Augustine's when he was a student there. Antonio introduced C.J. to Trevor, and C.J. was impressed. I think C.J. arranged for us to meet "accidentally" to test our chemistry, and it worked. I'd never really experienced Trevor's level of technical expertise. (I don't want to put down my former coaches, who were great, but I had to start thinking bigger.) After that practice, Trevor and I had a chat, with C.J. there, and we agreed that I'd come out to Raleigh every day, Trevor would run me through workouts, and we'd see how it went. We didn't talk about formal coaching.

We quickly got into a rhythm. I'd go to the N.C. State track every morning, a 25-minute commute, and work out with Trevor and his three other athletes—there was Antonio and two other lesser-known guys. Then I'd go to the weight room on my own or with C.J. It was great. I'd been running all my life and had been around a lot of people who claimed to know about every aspect of track and field, so I wasn't easily impressed. But I was very impressed with Trevor. He was very knowledgeable about the sport, and we also hit it off immediately. I loved his laid-back Jamaican attitude because I don't like a lot of drama around me. Plus, he wasn't interested in being a father figure. I'd dealt with that tendency in past coaches—maybe because I'm a woman; maybe because they knew about my background and thought I might be missing a dad; or maybe it was just in their nature. But I didn't like it and I didn't need it. All in all, Trevor Graham was the perfect fit.

The methods Trevor taught for running the 100m were very specific, and at the time I believed they were 100 percent correct. Much later, I learned that his way wasn't the best for me. But for the entire five years I trained with Trevor, this is what I would do: He taught me to get my first foot down as fast as I could out of the blocks, to slam it on the ground and create power. The first steps out of the blocks, he said, should be short and powerful. His philosophy was that the 100m is broken down into three different parts. The first was the drive phase: powering out of the blocks from the start to about 25 or 30 meters in which you keep your head down and apply a lot of force. He'd always say, "Let me hear it, let me hear it!" meaning that he wanted my footsteps to be audible; he wanted a definite *boom-boom-boom-boom-boom* on the track. The aim of the drive phase was to begin to pick up speed, and it lasted for about the first 14 steps. Then came the transition phase, when he wanted me to bring my head up slowly and settle into my comfortable running position, ready for the next phase, the acceleration phase, which needs no explanation. By about 50 meters, I'd really be running. There was a fourth phase too, the deceleration phase. If you watch even world-record holders closely, you'll see they slow down over the last 10 meters or so, even if only by an infinitesimal amount. It's involuntary, of course—the body can only run at top speed for so long. Trevor wanted to limit that as much as possible, so he insisted that you should never lean into the tape. He believed that leaning makes your legs lose their power because your feet and legs rise up behind you toward your butt. I could never get that part down. As soon as you come to a big race and it's tight—trust me, you're leaning.

Ten short weeks later in Indianapolis, I had the chance to test what I'd learned at the USA Outdoor Track & Field Championships. It was the first time in three years I was competing against elite runners, and I couldn't *wait!* However exciting my first 100m race would be, what I was looking forward to most was the long jump because I would for the first time get to compete against Jackie Joyner-Kersee, who by that time was done with the circuit and was only competing at the nationals and worlds. I say "compete against," not meet, because I had actually met her once before at a meet in Spokane, Washington. And though I was only 10 years old at the time, I remembered her giving a talk to us kids, and me asking shyly for her autograph, like it was yesterday. Jackie was my idol. I had her in a whole different department in my mind from the other elite

▲ C.J. was a constant companion during workouts and a real support when I first began competing on the professional circuit.

◄ Trevor Graham, my former coach, and I talk about a workout.

HE TAUGHT ME TO GET
MY FIRST FOOT DOWN
AS FAST AS I COULD, TO
SLAM IT ON THE
GROUND.

athletes, and not only because of her great feats but also for her graciousness. For the others I was about to race against, I used my old tried-and-trusted self-motivation technique. I pictured them sitting around when I started playing college basketball in 1993 breathing sighs of relief: "Good! We're done with her! She's out of our hair!" Now, I told myself, they were not happy. "Aww, shucks!" they were complaining, "She's back! We have to deal with her again!"

As it turned out, it probably wasn't such a far-fetched scenario. I was already under the microscope before the first heat of the 100m because it was my first comeback race at a championship meet since high school. Also, Trevor had gone out on a limb and predicted that, sometime this year, I was going to run a 10.76. *10.76!* That had been the world-record time until Florence Griffith Joyner clocked her 10.49 in 1988. Only she, Merlene Ottey and Evelyn Ashford had ever run a 10.76. Trevor's announcement (which was all his idea) may not have gone down too well. But when I beat Chryste Gaines and Inger Miller by a good stretch to win the 100m, I made a comment about how happy I was, having only started training 10 weeks ago. The comment went down like a slab of concrete. I hadn't meant to boast, but I think some of the ladies I competed against thought it was a brash thing to say. As far as I was concerned, I was just a young kid trying to run fast like everybody else. I'd only spoken the truth. Nowadays I try to measure the ramifications of what I say beforehand, but back then, despite those mind games I used to fuel my drive, I didn't seriously think anyone would dislike me, even if I said what was on my mind.

Unlike some of the other more senior athletes, Jackie Joyner-Kersee was a wonderful ambassador for track and field. I was completely in awe, but she wouldn't let me idolize her. One of my most cherished moments of my life was sitting next to her—the woman I'd been looking up to almost my entire life—not as a fan with my jaw dropped, but as an equal, as a competitor. She didn't talk down to me, nor look at me with mistrust, as a youngster who was trying to dethrone her. Winning didn't even matter to me at that point; I was just so thrilled to be able to tell my kids one day that I competed against the greatest ever. And maybe that attitude helped my performance, because I won. Afterward, Jackie was every bit as nice to me as she had been before—nicer in fact. She congratulated me and gave me encouragement and advice. "You have so much ahead of you," she said. "Be very, very careful whom you trust, because there are going to be a lot of people pulling you in every different direction." I have to confess I'm not at all sure that if I get to reach her stature in the track world in however many years, I'm going to be that nice to the young up-and-comer who just beat me!

Later on, after we'd talked a few more times at various functions and I'd got over being slightly tongue-tied, Jackie became the big sister to me that she is now. I remember admitting to her at one point that we'd first met a long, long time ago. "Oh, sure, I remember," she said, "You were that little girl in Spokane, Washington."

In 1997, I still had a lot of that 10-year-old girl in me—the one who was only interested in running her best and enjoying the experience, unconcerned with how she appeared to others. I can see how that led to some of my fellow competitors being unhappy with me, but I don't know what I could have done about it. I was immediately successful when I came back to track, and from the nationals onward, I was thrust into the limelight and called "the future of American female sprinting." It was a flattering label, but one I never asked for; it isolated me and put me into a different category. It was hard to develop any significant relationships with my fellow American sprinters, and I began to hear some of my competitors say negative things about me in interviews, on TV or through the rumor mill. It was frustrating because it wasn't as if I was out there giving everybody the bird, saying, "I'm taking over the world and I don't care whose toes I step on!" On the contrary, I was scrupulous about giving credit to my competitors in every interview—"So-and-so had a great start. So-and-so really pushed me to this time. . . ." I have always respected my fellow athletes more than I can say.

When we started traveling the European circuit, I found it could get very lonely out there, even though C.J. was with me. We are all simply competitors in Europe. We don't wear "USA" on our chest; we wear the names of our sponsors. But I still feel that the other Americans are my teammates, in a way. Some— Gail Devers springs to mind—were amazingly warm and supportive of me from the start; others were downright hostile. I don't expect to be best buddies with everyone; pleasantries will do, like the odd "Hi, how are you? How's your family?" but I found the Europeans were often friendlier than my fellow Americans. I wished for more camaraderie because I could have used some help figuring out how the circuit worked. Fortunately, I had C.J. watching my back. Early on, he introduced me to his agent, Charlie Wells of Vector Sports Management, whom I liked right away and with whom I signed a contract—I'm still with him today. From Charlie and C.J., I learned the ropes. But for most young athletes starting out, it's tough to find the most basic information about their new world. I always say I wish USA Track & Field, our governing body, had a mandatory "How to Be a Track Athlete" seminar for everyone who goes from college to the elite level of competition. It should tell you, "Okay, this is how you get paid. This is how to prepare yourself for taxes. This is how much an average managerial contract will cost you. This is what your manager will ask of you. This is the percentage your agent takes. This is how the money works in Europe. . . ." If you don't know all that, it's easy to mess up. You don't automatically get magazine covers and *Oprah* appearances when you run fast; you have to be in the right place at the right time, talking to the right reporters. It has to be mapped out for you. I was lucky because I was looked after, but I do think the "elders" of the U.S. track and field team ought to provide role models for the younger kids coming up. A self-serving, "show me the money" attitude, which some athletes display—a minority, admittedly, but a significant one—is so bad for the sport.

I don't mean to sound down about my early days traveling the circuit with Trevor and C.J., because I was in heaven. I was training hard, running fast and seeing my body change and get fitter. I was traveling the world and seeing all these great places, doing what I love doing: running and competing. And I was getting paid for it. That's a pretty life.

I was making prize money and also a small salary from my first contract with Nike—not much, but compared with college (i.e., practically zero) it was riches. My sponsorship duties then were to do some public appearances, compete in a certain number of track meets and, of course, wear Nike gear. There were provisions in my contract that if I ran a certain time or jumped a certain distance, I'd get bonuses. I easily fulfilled those competition obligations because I was going all over the place—to get my feet wet and to prepare for the biennial World Championships in Athens that summer, and because I wanted to. We (the team, which was Charlie, C.J., Trevor and me) went to some really small meets in Europe, in Zagreb, Croatia, for instance, and in Turin, Italy. In Croatia, I almost missed the starting gun because Serbo-Croatian for "take your marks" and "get set" sounds nothing like it does in English! In Turin, Italy, we warmed up in the park across the street from the track, and there were no real bathrooms in the stadium—just holes in the ground, which the athletes had to share with the crowd. I remember standing in line with track fans in front of and behind me, then bracing myself with both my hands on the wall, desperate not to fall into that big hole. Those were memorable experiences, all right.

▲ *Winning the 100m at the 1997 USA Outdoor Track & Field Championships in Indianapolis marked my successful return to sprinting full-time. I loved this haircut.*

▲ *The 1997 World Championships in Athens was my first real test against the best 100m sprinters on the professional circuit.*

But my confidence was building and I was learning a great deal about how this circuit was going to work for me. And it wasn't all tiny meets. I also took part in the big ones, running against the elite sprinters, getting accustomed to the pressure, because when a race was close I was still prone to revert back to what I knew. One time—I think it was in Oslo, Norway—I was neck and neck with Gail Devers, who was running in the middle lane next to mine, and I was intent on winning. I lost my good form and started to lean and pump my arms out to the sides. At the finish line, I realized my arms had been scratched up from Gail's long fingernails. When it happened a second time in the next race, we all had a good laugh and our managers resolved to make sure we were never put in adjacent lanes again.

That whole spring and summer, I was like a kid in a candy store. Not just because of the running, but also the sightseeing. I was getting to visit all these incredible places. I was supertourist. As soon as we landed somewhere, off I'd go with my camera strapped around my neck (in fact, I also took pictures out the plane windows *before* we landed). I still have the photos: the Brandenburg Gate, the Eiffel Tower, Big Ben, the Colosseum. Sadly I can't do that any more, especially in Europe, unless I take a bodyguard. Sometimes I feel embarrassed by the guards, managers, coach, camera crew, soundman and so on who tend to be with me wherever I go. I don't want schoolkids, for instance, to get the idea that I'm unapproachable, because I'm not. The entourage allows people to get the idea I think I'm all that, but it's not my idea—it's simply expedient or part of an obligation. Anyway, back in 1997, I was roaming free. And that year was a total eye-opener.

Another thing that started in 1997 after Indianapolis was me getting tested more frequently for performance-enhancing drugs. I'd been tested before. My name was on the testing list in high school because my times compared with those of the elite athletes and I ran at the National Championships. Once you'd been notified, you had 48 hours to give your urine sample to a registered lab and have it sent to USA Track & Field, so my mom used to take me out of school on certain days, and we'd drive two hours to the lab in Los Angeles. Mom was nervous we might miss such important notifications—we were in our apartment in Camarillo at the time—so she had those packages sent to coach Elliot Mason at his L.A. Harbor College. In 1993, one of the packages got stuck in the college mailroom for three days. By the time Coach Mason retrieved it, I'd already received a letter suspending me from the sport. It was horrible. It wasn't as if I was trying to cheat or avoid the test for any reason, but they wouldn't listen to my side of the story. So there was my name in the papers: banned, at 17 years old. Luckily, Mom had the idea of hiring the well-known attorney Johnnie Cochran, whom she knew of through her work. She wanted to send a message that we were serious; that they weren't just dealing with some single mom and her kid. And it worked. Mr. Cochran managed to get me out of the ban. But as soon as people read your name and the word "steroid," they don't read any further. The whole experience left a really bad taste in the mouth. And it didn't make the difficult time I had at Thousand Oaks any easier.

I got over the bad associations because both C.J. and I were asked to test for drugs more and more frequently. The routine went like this: At the lab, I showed ID, went to the bathroom accompanied by a female official and urinated into a cup. The urine was checked to make sure it wasn't too acidic or watered down, then sent off for testing. Testing for drugs is just part of your life if you're an athlete—and the better you get, the bigger the part. I was happy to take as many drug tests as they wanted.

Those tests, those meets, big and small, were all leading up to one major event in August 1997, the World Championships in Athens, where I'd be competing in the 100m, the 4x100m relay and the long jump. The World Championships is held every other year, and it's the big one. If you ask around, many track athletes might even tell you they prefer it to the Olympics, because it's just about us. At least half the crowd in the stands at the Olympics are there for other sports or for the spectacle itself, but for the World Championships, the devout, hard-core track and field groupies make a special pilgrimage. It also shouldn't be confused with the annual World Cup. That meet is a lot less competitive, because only one athlete from each region is permitted to compete. It's entirely possible at the World Cup 100m for a 10-point-something second sprinter to line up with seven women who can barely run 11.30, so it just doesn't have a lot of weight. My first world championships was unquestionably the biggest test of my life until that point, and I put my tourist activities on hold. For the first time that year, I did no sightseeing whatsoever, not even the Parthenon. I had to focus.

Probably because of my one-track mind at the time, my memories of Athens itself are few. I remember a chaotic city, thick with people and traffic and smog. It was hot, but far from unbearable, and the stadium was packed with thousands upon thousands of people. I had no doubt that I was going to make the finals, so the early heats of the 100m were a formality. The first clear memory I have occurred right before the final. Believe it or not, I remember my hairstyle. I'd had all my hair cut off back in college during my off year when I'd been really down, and I loved it so much that I'd kept it short. It was right for me at the time. It felt streamlined and cool. We lined up in the blocks, waited for the gun, and then . . . someone false-started. That was my first exposure in a major competition to a false start and the extra pressure it contributes. I was the youngest in the race, the outsider, and all too aware of how big this race was for me. I was already nervous, or perhaps excited, and the false start prolonged the agony. Then the wait became excruciating when Merlene Ottey didn't hear the second gun that signals the runners to return to the blocks and she ran 50 or 60 meters before she realized her mistake. She did exactly what I would have done in her shoes and took *forever* to walk back—it seemed like a good five minutes. So by the time we were ready to go again, I was probably more keyed up than I'd ever been in my life.

I don't remember running the race. I only remember winning. I ran my victory lap with tears streaming down my face, overcome with emotions. Here I was—finally—exactly where I'd always wanted to be. I'd been to college and played basketball and recovered from injury, and I'd graduated and come back to doing what I loved. So many people had doubted me, thought I'd never get to this position. I myself had not been sure I could make it. I knew I could run well and post fast times, and my confidence had been building, but I didn't really know how I would do under extreme pressure, whether I'd revert back to my old ways and fall short of the mark. Yet I'd made it. On that particular day I was the fastest woman in the world.

And that is why Athens will always have a special spot in my heart, even though I barely know the place.

After that I wanted to keep on running, but I encountered an unexpected rule of Trevor Graham's training philosophy. He believed athletes should take an entire month off after the season was over. No exceptions. This was a challenge. It was almost a greater challenge than the one I'd just faced in Europe. I bugged him with phone calls: "Are you *sure*, Trevor? Can't I even go for a little jog?" I wasn't used to inactivity

I WAS THE YOUNGEST IN THE RACE, THE OUTSIDER, AND ALL TOO AWARE OF HOW BIG THIS RACE WAS FOR ME.

(Clockwise from top of opposite page:) September 1998: press conference prior to the IAAF World Cup, Johannesburg, South Africa; September 2000: IAAF Golden League Athletics Meeting, Olympic Stadium, Berlin, Germany; August 1998: IAAF Golden League Monaco Hercules Zepter Grand Prix, Stade Louis II in Monaco, Monte Carlo; July 1998: Goodwill Games, Mitchell Field, Long Island, New York; May 1998: Prefontaine Classic, Hayward Field, Eugene, Oregon; June 1998: U.S. Track & Field Championships, Tad Gormley Stadium, New Orleans, Louisiana; September 1998: IAAF World Cup, Johannesburg Athletics Stadium, South Africa; July 1998: Goodwill Games, Mitchell Field, Long Island, New York; June 1998: U.S. Track & Field Championships, Tad Gormley Stadium, New Orleans, Louisiana.

DURING THE 1998
SEASON, HE COMPETED IN
37 EVENTS AT 27 MEETS
ON FIVE CONTINENTS.

for no good reason. I was afraid of losing all the hard work I'd put in. Also, sitting around like that was raising ghosts from that terrible, all too recent year of injuries. I couldn't wait for the month to pass so I could get back in training, lose the weight I'd gained that October and plan my next year of competition.

The *plan* for 1998 was for it to be a year of consolidation. Even more than that, I saw it as a year to push myself harder than I ever had before. I wanted to do everything, go everywhere, see all the places I'd dreamed of—and compete in them at the highest level. After my victory in Athens the year before, I was the best in the world; there was no way I could see a possible challenge ahead and *not* meet it. I was going to use the season to compete around the world, make money and gain exposure. And since there was no World Championships or Olympics in 1998, there was no reason to hold anything in reserve for a big finish. We sat down—Trevor, Charlie and I—and drew up a schedule. Once we'd gotten it down and planned it out, I didn't stop to think about what I'd let myself in for. I would consult the list, see what was next and off we'd go. During the 1998 season, I competed in 37 events at 27 meets on five continents.

Of all those meets, the one I was most interested in was Sydney. I didn't publicize the fact (except to Athletics Australia, which sponsored my visit), but I wanted to preview the Olympic city, to get acclimated, to see what I could of the site and get used to being there so that nothing could throw me come 2000. We spent a whole month in Australia, and I totally fell for the country. I loved the weather and had a great time training and competing there. And the Australians are so friendly—I adored them, as everyone does. But the city I loved the most was Melbourne. It was more suburban than Sydney, a place where people choose to live their whole lives. It reminded me of Raleigh. Also, the meet I competed in there was fun. It was so low-key it was almost quaint, attended by a manageable, all-local crowd of about 10,000.

I also liked Sydney, though it was so much bigger and busier. I trained hard and scouted accommodations for myself, my team and my family for 2000 because I already knew I didn't want to stay in the Olympic village. But the highlight of the visit was definitely my tour of the Olympic site. The Australian 400m sprinter, Cathy Freeman, who was a friend by that time, came with me, and neither of us could wait for our visit inside of what would become Stadium Australia. It was only a building site at that point, but it was easy to see where everything was going. I stood on the track where the 100m would be and slo-o-wly took it all in, gazing up at the framework for the stands, trying to visualize myself two and a half years in the future, running right there in that lane with 100,000 people watching. Talk about meaningful moments.

Aside from Australia, one of my favorite places to run is China. I'd been there in high school to play basketball, but in 1998 I went back in very different circumstances—to take part in a special "Fastest Woman" competition in Chengdu. They say it's better to travel hopefully than to arrive—but not that time. My usual team plus a few other American athletes were taking a China Airlines flight from Europe—I forget from where we left, but it was someplace very hot—and there was some problem with our group that prevented us from boarding. Charlie finally sorted it out and they let us on the plane, where we found a full load of passengers who had been strapped in for two hours, held on the runway in the boiling heat because of us. They were angry. If you've never had 200 Chinese people glaring at you, it's hard to understand how scared we felt. But we swallowed hard and proceeded to climb over their feet, scrambling for the few available seats that hadn't been assigned. After takeoff, it gradually dawned on C.J. and me that these people weren't just

◄ *Running the 100m in August 1998 at the IAAF Golden League Zurich Witklasse Grand Prix at the Letzigrund Stadium in Switzerland.*

89

random passengers—they were Chinese sports reporters en route to Chengdu. I spent the rest of the flight fending off one journalist after another who were trying to fight their way through Charlie to grill me about my pending race against the local favorite.

This did not bode well for the meet. Often these special "Fastest in the World" kinds of races are sketchy. They're not necessarily very professional and their funding can fall through, leaving the athletes unpaid. But it turned out that our fears were completely unfounded. This meet was put together by the Chinese government in honor of the sprinter Li Xuemei, who had run an Asian record–breaking 10.79 the previous year. The meet itself was awesome, every bit as good as the European ones, well organized, with a perfect warm-up area and a packed stadium of crazed track fans. I loved that noisy, dusty city and we were treated royally, right down to a fantastic ceremonial banquet hosted by the mayor. Every minute of the experience was great . . . until I beat Li Xuemei, and the fans and the national press ate her alive. She was unprepared, they said. She'd let them down. The poor woman was in tears at the press conference after the race. I felt so bad for her that when we went back out to the track for the medal ceremony and I stepped onto the first-place platform, I brought her up there with me. The crowd roared and I think she felt a bit better. In all, it was a great experience. But afterward, I have to admit that I told my manager: "Charlie, if they do that meet again, let's find a better airline."

Another favorite memory that stands out from that season is meeting Nelson Mandela. I absolutely loved South Africa, maybe even more than Australia. When traveling in Europe, you can always tell where you are from the uniformity of the people and the culture around you, but everything was so diverse in South Africa, with people of every color and different cultural cues—and it was inspiring to see after all the troubles they've been through with apartheid. I found it really exciting. I also had the most incredible food, especially when we were driven out to the countryside around Cape Town. I was already happy with the experience in South Africa, but it got much richer still when Charlie called my hotel room to say someone from the government office was wondering if I'd care to meet Nelson Mandela. I was over the moon. Nelson Mandela! Nelson Mandela had asked to meet *me!* Would I like to meet him? What kind of question was that? Of *course* I'd like to meet him.

Immediately I called my mom back home to tell her; then I had a clothing crisis, but luckily it turned out I had brought one reasonably nice outfit just in case. I was driven up to the Mandela estate, and there he was, the great man himself. Immediately, I was struck by the aura around him. He is a magnetic presence. He radiates positive energy and makes everyone in the room feel wonderful. I thought about how this man had spent 27 years behind bars, yet he managed to come out with a total absence of bitterness and with his unique spirit intact. I found him playful, almost childlike in the obvious joy he took in life. That level of charisma is such a rare quality, something I'd only come across once before—when I met Muhammad Ali. The other thing about Mandela that struck me right away was his hands. He has the most enormous hands— he used to be a boxer—with a viselike grip. I have no idea what I said to him; I was so awestruck I'm sure I mumbled something incoherent. He told me, "I'm a big fan, and I wish you the best of luck." Then we stood for photos—the sprinter Michael Johnson was also there, plus a couple of other people—and he was right next to me in all of them. (As it turns out, he's a bit of a ladies' man!) I have pictures from all over the world, but it is those shots of me with Nelson Mandela that I treasure the most. It was altogether one of the best experiences of my life, and it eclipsed the competition that took me to South Africa in the first place.

I HAVE NO IDEA WHAT I SAID TO HIM; I WAS SO AWESTRUCK I'M SURE I MUMBLED SOMETHING INCOHERENT.

▶ *Florence Griffith Joyner's death came as a shock to me and the rest of the sports world. Here she is running at the 1988 Seoul Olympic Games.*

The meet in South Africa was the last of the season, the World Cup in Johannesburg. I think I was a little exhausted by this time, not from running but from traveling. I wanted to go home. Dreary 70-degree weather and the city's altitude were getting to me, too. It's true, I managed good times, personal bests in fact—a 21.62 in the 200m (the third-fastest ever) and 10.65 in the 100m. By the time the long jump came around on the last day, it was raining, and 20 degrees cooler, and I guess my heart just wasn't in it. The great German long jumper, Heike Drechsler—another competitor who has always been sweet and generous to me, no matter who beat whom—took the lead early on. My best jump was still three inches behind hers when I fouled at my last attempt and lost.

That marked my first loss of the season. I was disappointed, sure, but I was so looking forward to having some time at home so I didn't take it too hard. Looking back on that 1998 season, I think of what a great time it was. Chaotic, insanely so at times, but an unmatched experience. People said at the time, "Why are you putting yourself through those hoops a second year in a row? Why do you keep running all these meets?" But to me there was no other option. I was 22 years old, possibly at the peak of my fitness, and I loved to compete above all things—so if not now, when? And I'm so very glad I did it because there's no way I'll be able to keep to that schedule ever again. It was the chance of a lifetime.

C.J. and I got home in September and had a few days of blissful relaxation before a piece of bad news hit. I got a call from Trevor. Had I heard? Florence Griffith Joyner had suddenly died at the age of 38, apparently from a heart seizure. "Shocked" doesn't begin to describe how I felt when I heard the news. I was struck dumb. I didn't understand how it could possibly happen—and not only did it happen, but people were responding to the news in the vilest fashion. Florence hadn't been gone 24 hours before the media started treating her family and her death with such disregard, such dishonor. All those years they could have challenged Flo-Jo's thus far untouchable records, but they waited until she could no longer speak up for herself. The charge was, of course, that she'd been taking performance-enhancing drugs, and now it was left to her grieving family, especially her widower, Al, to defend her. It was so unfair.

I guess one expects that kind of hard reaction from the media, but what got me down in particular was how the governing body of her own sport did nothing to defend Florence. I believe USA Track & Field put out some brief statement, but why they couldn't have stepped up and said something positive in her defense, I'll never know. To put it mildly, she was one of the all-time greats of this sport, and they did nothing to protect her reputation. It disheartened me and made me wonder, so what happens if *I'm* not running fast or if I retire from the sport or die or—yes, hopefully—break Flo-Jo's records? Will they turn their backs on me too? It's difficult to say this because I want to be patriotic, to win Olympic medals and have the Stars and Stripes flying and the national anthem playing. But Flo-Jo's death made me think that those who organize the sport in this country are maybe not there for us like they claim they are.

Of course, I called Jackie Joyner-Kersee as soon as I heard, and offered my family's condolences. She was off to California to help her brother, Al, and her niece, Mary Ruth, whom she's very close with. She too was saddened by the sport's general reaction. I confess I had an additional cause of sadness, a selfish one. I'd never met Florence, and now I never would.

10.49. 21.34. Those are the times that I strive for, that I run for, that are up in lights in front of me wherever I go. Those times, Flo-Jo's records for the 100m and 200m, respectively, are the reason that I compete. Sure, I love the competition for its own sake, but when you have a goal and you've had it for so long, you start to want it more than anything else. You start to need it. I'm on record saying I think it's possible for those records to be broken, and I stand by that. I intend to prove that it's possible. What annoys me is that you see the men constantly getting faster, but it seems the women are stuck. Why? Personally I can see lots of areas where I can improve, where I can make up time. But sometimes I wonder if my fellow competitors see it too, or if they're really, truly content with running 11-second 100m races. We have to do better than that at the elite level. People were running at those times in the 1960s. We should have evolved by now. We have better tracks. We have better footwear. We have better knowledge about vitamins. We have better coaches. We have better everything. Why are we still stuck at these mediocre times? It shouldn't be acceptable.

The depressing part is that it's now years after Florence set these records, and female sprinters still seem to shrug their shoulders and say, "Well, those will never be broken anyway. We're not going to even try to get close." They have their excuses: She was on drugs. She was wind-assisted (and, really, who cares whether the darn wind was stronger than what was recorded?) But I say, let's get out of this defeatist mind-set! It can be done. It *will* happen. For myself, I see that if I improve on certain things, those times are beatable. I'm not saying it's easy. It is not *easy*. I'm saying that everything would have to unfold perfectly for me to break those records. From the time I wake up that morning, everything would have to be just so: My eggs cooked the way I like them, the wind fair, my shoes broken in, the car ride, the media, the crowd . . . everything would have to go just right. But it can happen. It will happen.

# EVERYTHING WOULD HAVE TO GO JUST RIGHT TO BREAK FLO-JO'S RECORDS. BUT IT CAN HAPPEN. IT WILL HAPPEN.

SEIKO

6 LAN

◀ (previous page) The 2000 season began with a
long-awaited mission in mind: Qualifying and
competing at the 2000 Olympic Games in
Sydney, Australia.

▲ C.J. and I decided to keep our wedding in 1998
low-key. My brother, Albert, gave me away.

C.J. and I had plans for the training break after the 1998 season: our wedding. When we got engaged the previous spring, it had been low-key right down to C.J.'s proposal. He'd just returned from a meet in South Africa and we were sitting around at home when he casually asked me, "Do you want to get married?" Of course I said yes. I was in love—I thought this was what I wanted. After two crazy seasons in 1997 and 1998, it was practically the first time I could sit still, let alone pull off a wedding. We picked the date, October 3, sent out 100 invitations to family and friends, and hired a wedding coordinator. C.J. is a Muslim and I'm not a regular churchgoer, so we didn't want a church wedding. Instead, we found a banquet hall in Raleigh for the reception and had the marriage ceremony in the attached garden outside. I went gown shopping and asked my childhood friend Janelle Simon to be my maid of honor. Melissa Johnson, Tiffany Weatherford and Jessica Gaspar, my friends and Lady Tar Heels teammates, were also in the wedding. My uncle and cousin were flying in from Belize for the occasion, and Albert was going to give me away. On C.J.'s side, Trevor, my training partner Antonio Pettigrew, plus some other athletes were groomsmen and an old friend of his was best man.

I didn't involve my mom all that much in the wedding process. I was still being a little standoffish with her. From the start, she hadn't really approved of C.J. She never told me in so many words—she didn't need to. I knew she thought C.J. was too old for me, too brusque and brash. And she felt C.J. took me away from my family even more by hovering over me. I don't think C.J. ever caught on that she felt that way about him, but she couldn't hide it from me.

I was hardly the type of little girl to dream of a fairy-tale white wedding, so I didn't treat the day itself like the huge deal some people make it. But I did enjoy it, watching my friends and my family dancing and seeing everything going smoothly. Or almost everything. I found I could dismiss my mom's obvious discomfort because I was still in my rebellious phase. I was digging in my heels, metaphorically speaking: *Nobody can tell me who I'm going to marry. You don't understand him. You don't understand me. . . .* Yet Mom did blunt the joy of the occasion by being quiet all day. It was as if she was saying it out loud: This was not the way she'd planned for her daughter to be married. I found out later on that Albert also had concerns about C.J., but he's one of those people who gets along with anybody and everybody. He'd never let on if he had a problem with someone, and he'd never interfere or argue with his sister's decisions. All in all it was a wonderful time, but hardly the best day of my life, as people sometimes say of their weddings. (And the recent "best day of my life" had just happened in Athens in 1997.)

We skipped the honeymoon. All we wanted to do was stay home anyway, because of all the traveling we'd been doing for the past two years. And before we knew it, November arrived and training started up again in earnest—for C.J. too. His coach, Brian Blutreich, was in Chapel Hill, and I was still with Trevor at N.C. State in Raleigh. But things had changed in the 18 months since my introduction to Trevor's team. For starters, he'd picked up more athletes. There were eight or nine others out there as we approached the 1999 season. Also, our loose coaching arrangement had been formalized. Though it was his dream to train athletes, it was still just Trevor's daytime activity; he made his living working as a security officer at a pharmaceutical company called Glaxo Wellcome by night. Right through our first season together, nobody had even mentioned the issue of contracts or payment. But after the '97 season, Trevor realized I had some guaranteed income stemming from my success and from my new Nike contract. At the beginning of 1998, he'd asked if I could start paying him. Oddly, though, none of these arrangements happened directly between me and him. He roped in C.J. as a go-between.

With C.J. as a conduit, we sorted out the business side of things in 1998 and entered into a more formal coaching arrangement. As 1999 began Trevor announced—again through C.J.—that he wished he could devote more time to the group, but to do that he'd have to quit his job. I increased the amount I paid him. It was not an outrageous sum and I had no problem with his bringing other athletes into the group; he needed the additional income they provided. However, I did have a problem with some of the individual athletes. Trevor didn't do any research on the people he invited in, and some of them were disruptive. They'd complain constantly or they were what I'd call "bad apples," involved with the wrong crowd. I learned much later, some even got into trouble with drugs. Those characters would come and go, but one young lady who started in 1999, Chandra Sturrup, stayed on and became my good friend.

I liked Chandra from the very beginning. She was quiet and worked hard. She was from the Bahamas—and I have a certain affinity for people from the islands. We clicked. On the road, I had C.J., of course, but Chandra—who long-jumped and ran the 100m, the 200m and the 4x100m relay for the Bahamas—became my female companion, a road buddy as close as any of my Carolina teammates had been. She eased the isolation I'd always felt on the circuit from having been singled out and put on a pedestal. We'd go out, go shopping, have a good time. We had fun. And despite the occasional distraction, the athletes at N.C. State's Paul Derr Field practiced at a high level. It was a good training environment.

I started that 1999 season back in South Africa—not to compete this time, but to join several other elite athletes in opening a community center in Soweto. The International Association of Athletic Federations (IAAF) had asked me to do it, and I'd jumped at the chance to return to one of my new favorite countries and spend time with some young South African track fans. I did a clinic with the local kids and taught them drills. It's one of my favorite things to do, spend time with youngsters like that—and it's so much better when it's just me and the kids—as opposed to me, the kids and the media. When the cameras are there, kids tend to stiffen up and get distracted, but when we're alone they can be themselves and play, and I can do the same. It was an extraordinary experience, a wonderful way to start another packed season.

The pressure had increased since the previous season because 1999 would culminate in August at the World Championships in Seville, Spain. There's a World Cup every year, which, like I said, I don't count as a major test, but the biennial World Championships matter. We decided I would start slowly, unlike in the past two seasons. First, I ran the 400m at the Mount San Antonio College Relays (which we call Mt. SAC) near L.A.—a meet close to my heart for geographical reasons and sentimental ones—I've been running it since high school. In general, I dislike the 400m. It really takes it out of you because it demands every last molecule of oxygen stored in your muscles—it's an endurance sprint. When I was a kid in sixth grade, the coaches in my first track club warned us, "Okay, now, that 400-meter race, it's gonna hurt." That's when I developed a distaste for it. Before then, I was seemingly able to run forever. But ever since that warning, after about the first 250 meters, I'd look for the wall they told me I'd hit. You just hope that point comes as late in the race as possible, because afterward it's really hard to maintain your technique and composure. By the final 30 or 40 meters of a 400, my legs are shaking, my tongue's hanging out and the finish line is retreating like a mirage in the desert. It feels like I'm running backwards. That's why I don't run the 400m very often. However, I was intending to run the 4x400m relay in the Sydney Olympics, which meant I had to get in some practice at Seville and make sure to qualify at the 2000 Olympic trials in Sacramento next year. I'd run the 400m at Mt. SAC last year and intended to make it my annual major 400m race. It was loading the dice a bit, since

▲ I've always been very serious about my training. My focus was tested in 1999, when Trevor introduced a number of new faces to the training group.

▶ Chandra Sturrup, a Bahamian sprinter, joined our training group in 1999, and we quickly became friends. Here, she's running in an early heat for the 100m at the 2000 Olympic Games in Sydney.

AAF - FUN IN

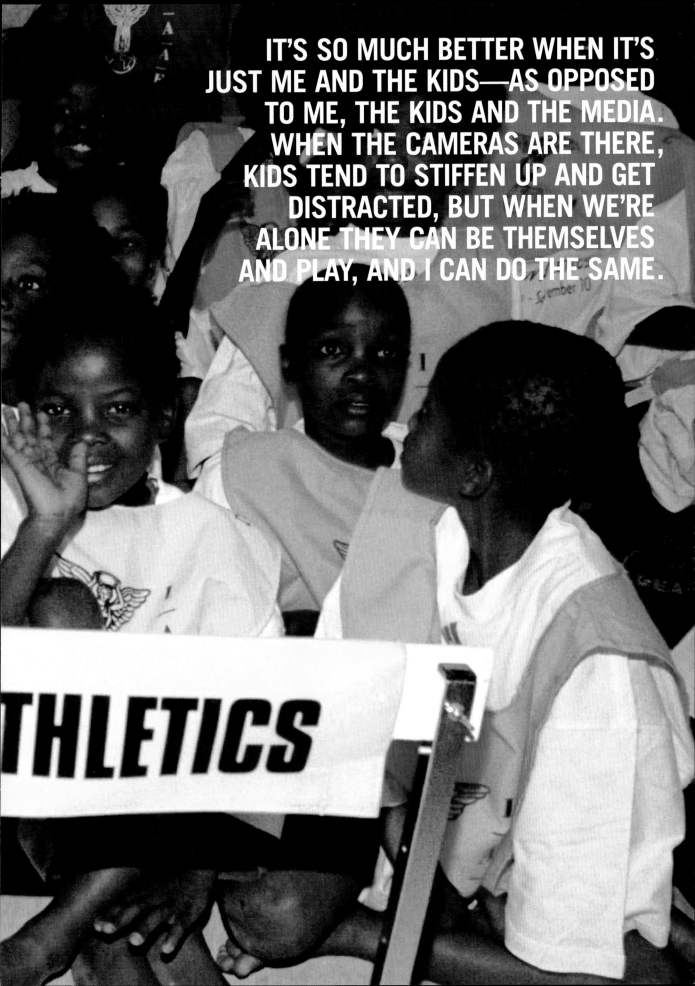

IT'S SO MUCH BETTER WHEN IT'S JUST ME AND THE KIDS—AS OPPOSED TO ME, THE KIDS AND THE MEDIA. WHEN THE CAMERAS ARE THERE, KIDS TEND TO STIFFEN UP AND GET DISTRACTED, BUT WHEN WE'RE ALONE THEY CAN BE THEMSELVES AND PLAY, AND I CAN DO THE SAME.

▲ It became apparent in 1999 that my unusual jumping style was risky. (top left to right, above) July 2000, U.S. Olympic Track & Field Trials, Sacramento, California; July 1998, IAAF Golden League Golden Gala, Olympic Stadium, Rome; June 2000, Prefontaine Classic, Eugene, Oregon; June 1999, U.S. Track & Field Championships, Eugene, Oregon. (Bottom) August 1999, IAAF World Championships, Seville, Spain.

most of the elite 400m sprinters skip Mt. SAC, but it was nice to post "the second-fastest 400m in 1999," as I eventually did . . . even if it got superseded in the record books within the month.

One of my next American meets was in mid-June, when the Pontiac Grand Prix Invitational took place right on my home turf in Raleigh, at Paul Derr Field. How could I not compete in that? It was a smallish meet, one of the events in an initiative dreamed up by USA Track & Field called the Golden Spike Tour. The idea of the tour was to offer American athletes enough meets here in the States to enable us to make money without having to go over to Europe. Or that was the ultimate aim, since 1999 was its first year. Our home track was soft, which was fine for training but too soft (i.e., slow) for competing. I didn't want to run there and post slow times, so I decided I'd just jump. To cut to the chase, after my fifth jump I was behind. Obviously, I couldn't lose on my home field, so I put my all into my sixth and final jump, and won. But thanks to my horrible—or let's call it unorthodox—style, where I slam rather than slide into the pit, I managed to jam my left knee so hard that it hyperextended slightly.

After ice packs, X-rays and MRIs, it turned out that my knee wasn't seriously injured. Even when I hobbled to Syracuse to stay with my good friend Melissa—a social visit that was such a rare opportunity for me I was determined to manage it—and my knee was inflamed so badly that Melissa had to ice it while I dangled my right foot in the pool and tried to have a good time . . . even then, I managed not to panic. And it turned out I was fine. But that accident brought on a whole new round of criticism from the media. They'd said it before, and they said it all over again: My jumping style was going to lead to a major injury. My mom told me recently that it used to tear her heart out to watch me jump from up in the stands because she'd always hear people around her drawing in their breath, exclaiming, "Oh, my God! Look at that! She's going to hurt herself!"

It was obvious to Mom and to the press that Trevor wasn't teaching me what I needed to know. In hindsight I see how it should have been obvious to me too, but it wasn't. When I've got your back, I'm the type who will be there for you until you stab me in mine—and I would have followed Trevor to the ends of the earth. He always admitted he wasn't a long jump coach, but he was willing to learn and said that we would evolve together. After the 1997 season, he had said, "Don't worry. We didn't concentrate on your jumping. We were just trying to get the running down." He was going to learn, he was going to consult with the best coaches and athletes in the world, and we'd make it happen. By the start of 1999, I assumed he had indeed studied the event over the winter. He did, after all, have new things to tell me. They weren't consistent things, but I didn't question that. I was too busy thinking: *Maybe it's me. Maybe I'm just not picking this up.* As for the media comments, well, I was beginning to mistrust the media anyway. They like to criticize. And my unorthodox style was working! Sure, it was ugly to watch and I was never sure if I was going to hit the board at all, let alone pull off a good jump, but that uncertainty brought possibility along with it. There was always a chance something great would happen.

Also, my rebellious spirit soared when I'd think of the other long jumpers saying: *Who does she think she is? She's so bad at this!* And then I'd beat them. But I was tiring of that in 1999. The German athlete Heike Drechsler—she and Jackie Joyner-Kersee are the two best female long jumpers in the history of the event—had taken me under her wing from the start, mentoring and mothering me in equal measure. From her and from Jackie I was getting over loving the sport for spite, and was beginning to see my enormous potential in it. I could be great at it, but I had work to do.

My knee healed in plenty of time for the World Championships, and I arrived in Seville feeling great. It was hot. Extraordinarily hot. I love heat and I'm used to it in Raleigh, but this was a whole other level.

Getting ready for the early rounds of the 100m, I also noticed right away that the track in the warm-up area was extremely hard, too hard to use. I did a few drills on it, then moved onto the grass. When I started running the actual heats, I discovered that the stadium track was just as hard. It was a surface made by Mondo—the Italian manufacturer that supplies nearly all the track for major competitions—but it must have been very thin and with concrete underneath it. Still, I ran fine through the first two rounds. Then I started to feel tightness in my back on the lower left side, a new and ominous sensation. I thought I must be dehydrated. But before I had to put any more pressure on my back, I got a chance to rest it in the stands and watch C.J. win the shot put gold medal—his first ever. That took my mind off the pain for a while. But it was back soon enough.

I always travel with a masseur or physiotherapist, but this time, in preparation for the extreme heat, Charlie Wells and Trevor had thought to bring a doctor, too, in case I needed an IV, plus a chiropractor and an acupuncturist. The last got my back loose enough for my semifinal the next day, though I could still feel twinges. Later that evening, I went into the final not feeling so hot. Inger Miller, with whom I have a long history and a chilly relationship, was in the final. She's from California, too, so we first ran against each other when I was a freshman in high school and she was a senior. During the '99 season Inger was at the very top of her form, and she was capable of upsetting me. Still, I pulled off a 10.70 and beat her. The following day I had the long jump final, which I barely remember, but I must have jumped reasonably well because I came in third. Afterward, my back was killing me, thanks to my unorthodox style.

Next up was the 200m, my favorite distance. I always look forward most to the 200m. But the day after the long jump, which was the morning of the first two heats, I could hardly get out of bed. It hurt to cough. I got every treatment available on my back—the chiropractor manipulated it, the IV hydrated it, the acupuncturist stuck needles in it—but it wouldn't loosen up. Nevertheless, I got through the first two rounds somehow and was in the semifinals the following day. The final was two days after that, so at least I'd have time to recover.

I must admit that acting is a secret skill of mine. It comes in handy whenever I'm hurt. If the media gets the notion that I might be injured, it spreads like wildfire. If I had a slight limp or a pained expression in the warm-up area, I'd be asking for trouble. Just the news of it would get me hounded by reporters, but it could also boost my competitors' and their coaches' confidence, giving them just the edge they need. We can't take that risk, so every single member of my camp is sworn to secrecy. I've gone through a number of massage therapists in my career—they like to talk! But even a casual bar chat or a polite answer to someone's question poses a danger—particularly in Europe, where "athletics" is much bigger news than it is back home. So, if I tweak my hamstring on the road and need to find an ultrasound machine, it's a problem. It had happened just before Seville, in fact, in Malmö, Sweden, which is no metropolis. Charlie had taken care of it, as usual, covertly finding a translator, explaining how it had to be hush-hush, and having him track down a physiotherapist. Luckily, the doctor didn't know track and hadn't heard of me. Between him and my masseur at the time, Marvin Finger, who introduced me to the magic of magnetic therapy, my leg was rehabbed. This type of subterfuge is easier when I avoid the athletes' dining hall, which is not hard to do. Like I said, I'm uncomfortable at being singled out; I had learned to keep myself to myself, and by 1999, sticking to my hotel room was an ingrained habit. There'd been a snowball effect: The more I kept away from the other athletes, the more snotty I seemed, so the more they kept away. There are plenty of places on the circuit I've been to for six years now, and I still don't even know where the dining hall is located.

◀ I was in the stands to witness C.J. winning the 1999 shot put World Championship in Seville, Spain.

▶ C.J. cut an imposing figure on and off the field. Here he prepares for a throw during the 1999 World Championships in Seville, Spain.

It was a boiling hot Spanish summer's day for the 200m semifinals. I gritted my teeth and acted nonchalant as I warmed up. It was agony. My back was so tight, I could barely walk. Still, I figured I had to take the chance, try to get through one race, then just one more after that—because if an injury rumor makes things hard for me, imagine what quitting would do. I wasn't worried about posting a bad time. I knew that if I could race at all, I was going to win. I might kill myself in the process—I might pass out—but if I could reach the finish line at all, I would reach it first.

As I left Trevor for the track and rounded the curve to the start of the 200m, I was by no means confident. I didn't know what would happen—it was one of the most uncertain moments of my whole career. Every time I put my foot on the ground, my back cramped up in a fierce spasm. I set my blocks and did some pop-outs, but it felt so horrible I left it at that and decided to do without my complete routine. At the gun my back was tight, but I told myself, *Okay, this could work.* . . . I was still going as I reached the curve, but then coming off it onto the straightaway—which is where I normally make my move—it all went wrong. I wasn't quitting, but my back had other ideas. Something in there balled up into a knot, as if to say, *Oh, no, you don't. You're not doing this,* and I doubled up in excruciating pain, lost control of my body so badly that I couldn't prevent myself from falling forward onto the track. Game over.

As a big, intimidating guy, C.J. was always an expert at barging through security when necessary, and he was with me in seconds, out on the track and picking me up along with the emergency medical people, who gave me a shot to relax the muscle spasm. Then my mom materialized—she traveled to the bigger meets—and Trevor, who was in tears. He felt he'd made the wrong call, that he should have prevented me from running. Later he told me he was fully responsible for what happened. But regardless of the pain, I doubt I would ever let him pull me out of a race I had even the faintest chance of completing. The acupuncturist went to work on me back in the room, but was unable to get even those long, tiny needles in because the muscles were so rigid and I was shaking so much. My Seville was over.

When my back finally eased up enough, I got on a plane and headed home. It was then that I realized my whole season was over. Something clicked. I saw how badly I needed a break. I saw how my life in the fast lane had sped up a little *too* fast. I'd had too much going on in Seville. I'd brought too many people with me. It was overwhelming, chaotic. I vowed never to make that mistake again.

Seville taught me a valuable lesson, but the disappointment from it was chronic. I'd been running so well. I was getting better competition than I'd ever seen before. And I still hadn't won a 200m world title. Not only that, but I hadn't won anything major in the long jump either. Here I was entering 2000, the biggest year of my career, and all I had done was win the 100m world title twice.

I made the most of the enforced time off. In 1998, C.J. and I had found a great getaway spot on Mustique, a private island in the Caribbean. We rented one of the magnificent villas there for two weeks and had the best time. Once I decide to stop, I really stop. I don't need a lot of activity on vacation. In fact, I don't want anything going on at all. Our villa was right on the water, with its own pool and people to cook and clean. We had picnics on the beach and ordered up anything we wanted for breakfast, lunch and dinner. I swim like a fish and love it, so I was in and out of the pool the whole time. C.J. and I were getting along famously. His career, of course, was at its peak, and he felt he truly deserved this vacation after his win at Seville.

◀ *My back had been hurting since I arrived at the August 1999 World Championships in Seville, but it wasn't until the 200m semifinal race that it spasmed uncontrollably and knocked me out of competition. C.J. was there to help me.*

By the time we got back home, we had two or three more weeks before training started, and my back was like new. I practically had to be held down to prevent me from heading for the track early. I was dying to get back into it. This was the big year. After saying no to the alternate's spot at Barcelona, and after the grievous disappointment of 1996, finally this was the year I'd been looking forward to my whole life.

I started training a week ahead of schedule. I'd done a lot of competitions in 1997, 1998 and 1999. This was what I was comfortable doing; this was what my body knew. We decided not to make changes by taking competitions off my schedule and running the risk of being uncertain at the trials in Sacramento or—God forbid—at the Olympics in Sydney, from lack of practice. I entered everything, from Mt. SAC and the Penn Relays to meets in Osaka, Rome, Zurich, Brussels, Berlin, Stockholm, London . . . you name it. We were confident that my body could withstand the aftermath of the injury in Seville. It hadn't been the result of overtraining or too many meets anyhow. It had been some unfortunate combination of the heat, the track and the chaos in my life. I knew I wasn't going to repeat that scenario.

As always Mt. SAC was the first meet of the season. As I said earlier, the elite 400m runners don't really get going until May or June, so Mt. SAC is my annual chance to post a good time in my least favorite event. In 2000, I aced it! I will always take pride in the fact that I held on to the world's fastest time in the 400m for, what, all of two weeks. My friend Cathy Freeman said later that hearing how I had run the best time in her event, the 400m, lent her extra motivation to come and take the top position away from me. I like to imagine that I helped her to win the gold medal in Sydney a few months later!

Of all the meets in the 2000 European season, Berlin is the one that stands out most in my memory. And it's not because I won the 100m in 10.78. Berlin was where C.J. went to get an MRI on his knee. When he returned, he was disheartened because he found out that he'd torn a meniscus and would be out of competition. I really felt for him, having myself been through the misery of missing the 1996 Olympics because of injury. In fact, the situation had me in tears. The bad news of his injury—and the fact that he wasn't able to train—put a strain on us. And in retrospect, I can trace a certain new tension in our relationship back to that time. It turned out that the injury was probably not foremost in C.J.'s mind. He had kept some crucial information from me. When he went for the MRI (and I assume that he really did go), he'd had a secret meeting with the IAAF to discuss the fact that he had tested positive for a banned steroid. When I found that out (and the meeting with the IAAF part of the story only came to light very recently), it was a slap in the face in so many ways.

First, I *always* like to know everything that's going on around me. I can understand why Trevor (who knew) and Charlie (who probably knew) kept quiet, because back then they thought I liked to be spared from any drama. But my husband? C.J. knew me. He certainly realized I'd want to be in the loop, yet he kept the truth from me. In fact, I'm not convinced that his knee problem was even all that serious then. Later on he had surgery, but in Berlin I'm not even sure if he saw a doctor. In other words, it's possible he flat-out lied.

Since then, I've agonized plenty about what could have been going through C.J.'s mind. It's obvious that he must have been ashamed. But I was his *wife!* I trusted him, and he should have trusted me enough to let me know what was going on—even if only so that I'd be prepared. As it was, when the truth came out in Sydney, I was still totally unaware. Yet, even then, he maintained that the news he'd tested positive was a compete surprise to him, that he didn't know how this could happen.

◀ Leading up to the 2000 Olympics in Sydney, I had more notoriety than anticipated because of my "five golds" prediction, which made me a popular cover girl.

▶ Despite all the attention on me and C.J. surrounding the games, I tried to find a sense of humor in it all, occasionally mugging for the cameras.

▲ Rounding the curve during the 200m final at the Olympic trials in Sacramento, California, leading up to the 2000 Olympic Games.

◄ Jackie Joyner-Kersee has been a friend and mentor since I started competing. She always had me cracking up at competitions, which she did again at her last one, the 2000 U.S. Olympic trials in Sacramento.

At the time, however, I was in a state of blissful ignorance. And despite the aforementioned tension and the sadness of C.J. not being able to compete alongside me in Sydney, it really was blissful. My season went very well. Olympic fever was mounting. My PR team was in overdrive. Before the start of the season, we'd sat down and mapped it all out. For months I'd been having a weekly conference call with selected reporters, plus a monthly "media day" when I'd be available in Raleigh for people to watch practice and to interview, film or photograph me. I'd long lost count of the magazine shoots and television interviews. It was added pressure, but it was wonderful pressure. By the time July rolled around and the Olympic trials had finally arrived, I was beside myself with excitement.

To make everything even more perfect, the trials were in California. They were in Sacramento, which is, admittedly, a ways from where I grew up, but any return to California feels like a homecoming to me. Being happy in that environment was a blessing. Despite my confidence, and despite being the favorite, I needed *some* level of comfort. This was, after all, my biggest competition yet by far. All the talk about Sydney, all that fuss about the five golds, would be for nothing if I didn't perform well at the trials.

Sacramento was hot. Boiling hot. As hot as Seville. And there was no shade. This was challenging, very challenging. My mom and my brother were there, naturally, along with lots of my friends from California, and my old coach from Thousand Oaks, Coach Brown. The meet was incredibly well organized and the crowds were jubilant. It was a marvelous atmosphere. The first event was the 100m, which I won with no problem. That qualified me for the 4x100m relay, and I was confident I'd be chosen for the 4x400m team. Speaking of relays, even though I'd made the infamous "five golds" announcement—or rather, I'd articulated my goals for Sydney—I should never make it sound like I choose which relays to run, because that's not how it works. The relay teams are selected by the coaches. I was pleased I had a place on the 4x100m team, but I was looking forward far more to joining the 4x400m team. Frankly, my 4x100m teammates and I (it's usually the same five or six sprinters) have never really clicked. Not being a fan of drama, I find the jockeying for position, the gossip and the difficulties setting up practices that take place with this group very trying. There's no chemistry—and that can lead to problems with baton passing. On the other hand, I've had nothing but delightful experiences running with the women who are normally assembled for the 4x400m. They're open and friendly, and there's no—and I'll come right out and use the word—*jealousy,* because I don't run their event. Other countries' relay teams train together year-round and know each other well, but we do not. I figured if the stress level with the 4x100m rose too high in Sydney, I'd just remember: This one's for America. . . .

The 200m race was significant for me, because I was still looking to win a big event at my favorite distance. For some reason, USA Track & Field saw fit to put the semifinals and the final less than an hour apart. Not only that, but they placed Inger Miller—who was still running very well at the time—and me in the same semifinal. Which was ridiculous—the two top runners should only meet in the final. To win my semifinal I had to run under 22 seconds in that intense heat. Then I had to come back 55 minutes later and do it again. Absurd. But it went fine. To win my first major 200m, I posted a time of 21.84.

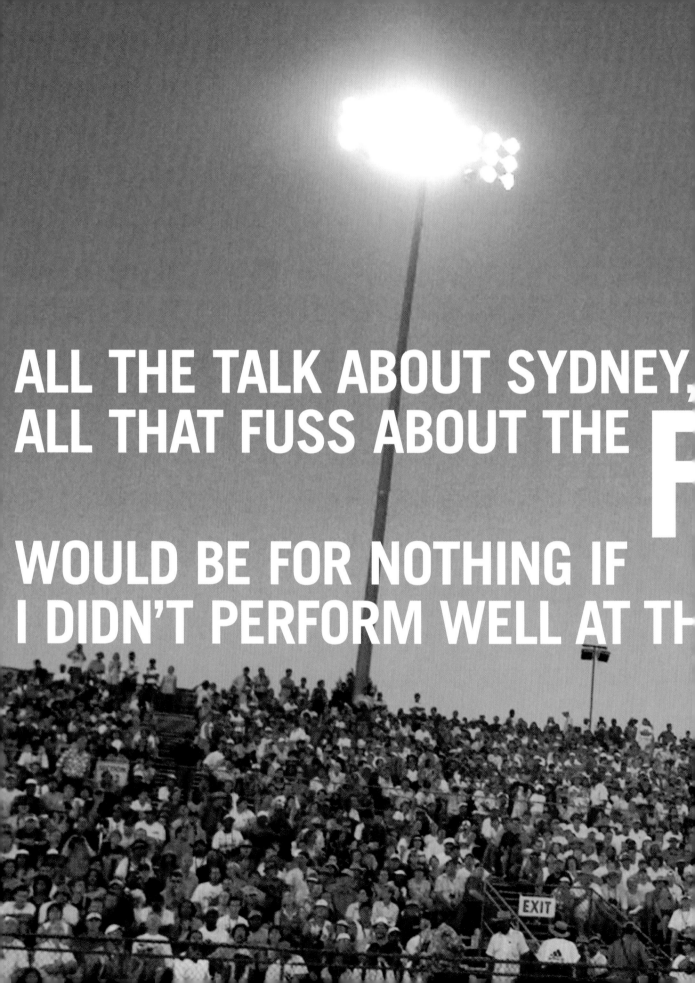

ALL THE TALK ABOUT SYDNEY,
ALL THAT FUSS ABOUT THE F

WOULD BE FOR NOTHING IF
I DIDN'T PERFORM WELL AT TH

In a way, the long jump was even more important to me than the 200m. Once again, I was going to get the chance to compete against Jackie Joyner-Kersee. Although my hero—and by then, a close friend and mentor—had announced her retirement, she'd decided to come back and try for one last Olympics. If she made it, Sydney would be her fifth. By 2000, my fourth year of competition, and Jackie being out of the picture, the tables had turned: I was the established athlete at the top of her game, and Jackie was the one facing a potentially career-altering challenge.

Normally, I race through competitions; I just want to get them done. But this time, I sat on the bench and took in the moment, watching the great woman jump. Regardless of whether she made the team or not, it was wonderful to witness. In between our jumps, we shot the breeze, the same as we always did. Wherever we competed together over the past years, Jackie would always lighten the mood. We'd chat about the silliest girl stuff—how she didn't like her outfit or how my uniform wasn't fitting right. The mood was set between us way back in Athens, in my first major championship. I have a picture from there that I treasure, of Jackie and I at the long jump runway after we've both put in poor performances. She's just said something about how horribly we did, and I'm laughing, and we both have this look on our faces that says, *Hey, we are stinking up the joint.* Jackie could always relieve the tension at a big-time competition.

But it wasn't her day in Sacramento. I sat on the bench and watched her run through the pit on her final jump, foiling her bid for one more Olympic medal. Then I did the exact same thing—except that my previous jump, my fifth , at 23'½", had been the longest of the day. I'd made it. I was on the way to my dream.

I had just witnessed my idol, the greatest ever, compete in her very last competition. But it wasn't a sad occasion. Jackie was done with competing. It was time, it was okay. Needless to say, she congratulated me warmly and wished me luck. "I'll be there in Sydney, cheering you on from the stands," she said. "No matter what, you'll always have a fan in me." It was the nicest thing I'd heard all year.

# MY JUMP HAD BEEN THE LONGEST OF THE DAY. I'D MADE IT. I WAS ON THE WAY TO MY DREAM.

# 7.FIVE
# BEH

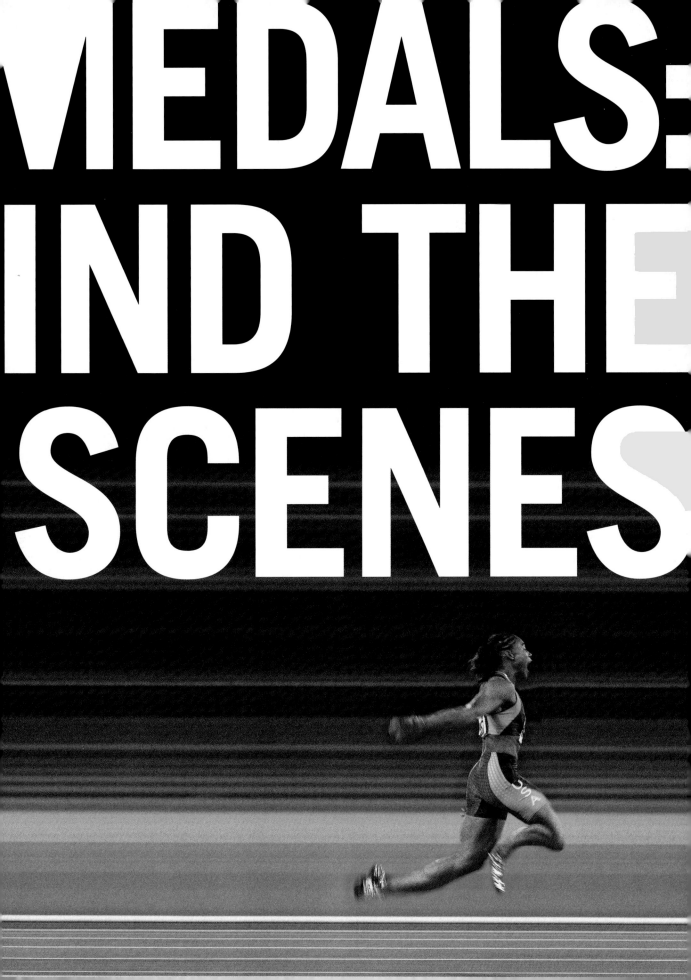

◄ (previous page) Me winning the 100m final at the 2000 Sydney Olympic Games. It didn't feel like I was anywhere near this far ahead.

▲ Among my greatest memories of the 2000 Olympic Games was being a part of the opening procession with Team USA.

◄ Even before we entered Stadium Australia, I was overwhelmed at meeting so many fellow athletes and coaches, among them Tommy Lasorda.

I slipped into Sydney virtually unnoticed. We'd been in Melbourne for two weeks, training in peace while I got over jet lag and waited out the Olympic arrival chaos. By the time we got to Sydney, most of the big-name athletes were already in town and the reporters had given up the Kingsford-Smith Airport vigil. Better still was our police escort, which slipped us through the back way so we didn't even have to wait for our baggage. It was fabulous—as was the apartment Charlie and I had found back in 1998. It was close to the stadium, but still far enough away from all the Olympic madness that I'd be able to stay peacefully out of the fray. (Or that's what I thought. Fate, as it turned out, had other plans.) I decided early on that I didn't want to be in the Olympic Village. There were so many horror stories about athletes staying up late partying. I didn't want to risk the distraction, especially in my first Olympics when I needed to be so focused. Maybe I was missing out, but I wasn't one to congregate with the crowd on the circuit anyway. And I wasn't about to change my solitary ways for the most important meet of my career.

However, I definitely wanted to participate in the opening ceremony. I wouldn't have missed it for the world, even though it was a lo-o-ng evening of standing around. We couldn't see the dance and music extravaganza in Stadium Australia from the arena where all the athletes waited to march in the Parade of Nations, but that didn't bother me. We had our own spectacle. Imagine representatives from nearly all the countries of the world congregated in one place, nearly 11,000 of us

in different colorful uniforms. One by one, the nations departed. Greece, in pale blue and white, led off. For the first time, North and South Koreans marched together and got a huge roar from the capacity crowd. Dusk turned into night long before the U.S. was called. With 602 of us, we were the second-biggest squad and the penultimate team to enter the stadium, just before Australia.

The waiting was almost the best part. We were soon all walking around and mingling. It was a thrill meeting athletes from other sports for the first time. I finally got to talk to Venus and Serena Williams. I love tennis, and I've been a fan of theirs since they started playing professionally. When I saw them, I just went up and said hi to introduce myself—they both knew who I was. Serena was really nice, very genuine and friendly. She said she was a fan of mine, too. But Venus . . . the first thing out of her mouth was, "You made the cover of *People* magazine before I did." I'm usually quick with a witty response, but that caught me off guard. I sort of stammered, "Yeah. I don't—you know, I don't know," and wished them luck and moved on. It was odd.

I also hung out with the U.S. women's basketball squad for a bit. Lisa Leslie is a good friend. She's a fellow Nike athlete and is also from California; she used to high jump when I was running in the California high school state meets. Dawn Staley too—she has her own foundation and community programs in Philadelphia, so I usually see her when I go to the Penn Relays. Also there was Tina Thompson, whom I knew from the World University Games team in Colorado Springs the summer during college when I broke my foot. I was chatting with the girls when somebody called out, "Hey, Marion! I've been wanting to meet you!" I looked up and almost fell over. When Ira was alive, he and I would go together to many Los Angeles Dodger games, and I was as big a fan of the former manager, Tommy Lasorda, as I was of his team. Now he was in Sydney as the coach of the U.S. men's baseball team, and he was rushing over to meet me. Tommy Lasorda! And he said *he* was a big fan of *mine*.

It was so funny. There I was, completely in awe of the whole situation, and of all these great athletes and coaches, and yet people were coming up to *me*, saying, "Hey, Marion, I'm your fan. May I have your autograph?" So many people, from fencers to volleyball players to swimmers, that I was amazed. I wanted to say, "This is my first time here, guys. I haven't even done anything yet! What do you want *my* picture for?"

Finally it was time for the U.S. squad to go into the stadium, so we lined up in our white panama hats, the women in red jackets and Stars and Stripes scarves, the men in dark-blue suits and white shirts with Old Glory ties. It was simply incredible as we went in. There was a wall of sound from the 110,000 people cheering and screaming—every one of them, it seemed, popping the flash in their cameras. The patchwork ocean of athletes in their multicolored uniforms was milling about on what was to become the ultimate track in a few days' time. Loads of them had brought their own video cameras, but I was empty-handed. I didn't want to experience this through a lens. As we completed a lap of the stadium, then stood together in the middle, I gawked, a huge grin on my face, unable to absorb the whole overwhelming scene. I was glad not to worry about capturing it on film because it would've been impossible anyway. It was all about being there.

Then the moment the world had been waiting for happened: The runner emerged with the Olympic torch and circled the stadium. She was wearing a snow-white bodysuit that all but glowed, marking her as the very center of the world at that moment. It was Cathy Freeman, my friend. It was so unbelievably exciting to have someone I personally knew charged with this task of tasks. I was so proud of her. Later, she wrote in her book about how the experience felt from her perspective—how she was terrified she'd trip and extinguish the flame, how violently she was shivering, and how when she stood in a few inches of water in the cauldron, lighting the Olympic fire, she found herself hoping she wouldn't catch cold. But from where I was standing, she was about the coolest person I'd ever seen. I remember all the athletes being in awe. We were teary-eyed. To be there witnessing that event was something I'll never forget as long as I live.

The Games had begun.

Of course, I had a week before *my* Games would begin, starting with the first heats of the 100m, but a piece of news surfaced right after the opening ceremony that affected me. It was announced that Inger Miller would not be competing. This wasn't exactly a surprise; rumors that she was injured had been circulating for weeks. The news took me back to when I was a high school freshman and Inger, a senior at the time, beat me in the 100m at the Arcadia Invitational, then mysteriously got injured just before the statewide meet a few weeks later. Only now, instead of local and state competitions, it was the Olympic Games. Inger ran well at the trials, and the media had flocked around her. She had a platform, so what did she choose to say? "It's not going to be the Marion Jones Show [in Sydney]." When reporters asked me about her comment, I'd just say something like, "I'm going out there to try to beat everybody on the track regardless of who they are." I might have my own little jokes in private, but I wouldn't dream of bad-mouthing another athlete in front of the press. Yet Inger kept focusing on me. I was her personal vendetta. And now she was out of the race.

Still, Inger missing the Games wasn't just a grave disappointment to her; it affected other things. Though she and I didn't train together and weren't exactly the best of friends, we'd run several 4x100m relays as part of a team and knew how to hand off the baton to each other. Now someone else, someone new to me, would be running the third leg.

SHE WAS WEARING A SNOW-WHITE
BODYSUIT THAT ALL BUT GLOWED,
MARKING HER AS THE VERY CENTER
OF THE WORLD AT THAT MOMENT. IT
WAS CATHY FREEMAN, MY FRIEND.
## IT WAS UNELIEVABLE
## TO HAVE SOMEONE I
## KNEW CHARGED WITH
## THIS TASK OF TASKS.

◄ (previous page) The 200m final, my second
event, came shortly after the story broke about
C.J. Despite everything that was going on,
I managed to keep my focus and win the race.

▲ After winning the 100m final at Sydney,
I celebrated with an American flag and a
Belizean flag, which caused a silly controversy.

There wasn't much to occupy me during the long seven days before I started competing. I desperately wanted it all to start. Apart from other things, I wanted to stop hearing about my now infamous, semiaccidental "five golds" prediction. Carl Lewis was the latest to weigh in, saying something along the lines of "What are 'her people' doing putting her in that situation?" It's too much pressure. It's a mistake. What he said gave me a hollow laugh. I'd been such a huge fan of Carl Lewis growing up. I'd idolized him— as had 85 percent of the athletes competing alongside me then, I'm sure. But by the time I was running at the elite level, I noticed how everything that came out of his mouth was negative: He'd complain that the present-day athletes were reaping the benefits of his hard work; that he deserved more than he got; that the sport had let him down. It was all about the sport itself, nothing personal—until Sydney. But I was well acquainted with my old idol's feet of clay by then. When he said that about me I just shrugged: *Well, there goes bitter Carl again.*

Finally, the big day came. The opening ceremony had been such an otherworldly experience, more of a grand opera than anything to do with sport. So it wasn't until I left the warm-up area and passed through the gate to the track for the early heats of the 100m that I got a real sense of where I was. After finally arriving in that magnificent stadium, the first thing I did was seek out the exact spot where Cathy Freeman and I had stood in 1998, on my stealth Sydney visit. It was difficult to put the two scenes together, but when I looked up at the packed stands and imagined them as that bare, skeletal framework, it was as powerful a moment as I had had since I arrived in Australia. It captured not just those past two and a half years, but a lifetime of focus, drive, hopes and passions into the goal I needed to achieve here. I was so happy I'd seen the place in its raw state. I felt like I matured with the stadium—that I was born to be there.

As I said in the beginning, winning the 100m was every bit as wonderful as I'd always dreamed it would be. I was on cloud nine after the victory, my unforgettable first. I was planning on riding that high, then coming down in a day or two to ready myself for the assault on the next medals, the 200m and the long jump. But at that moment, I was sky high.

Later that night, I got a phone call. "May I speak to Miss Marion Jones?" asked a man's voice. It was very familiar, the voice, yet I couldn't place it. Hardly anyone had this number—only Trevor, Charlie and my family—and it wasn't any of them. They must have given it out—but they wouldn't do that.

"Who is this?" I asked.

The man said he was the president of the United States.

"Come on, Albert!" I said. "Quit fooling around."

"No, this is Bill Clinton. I'm calling to congratulate you on behalf of the United States of America. We're very proud of you."

Whoa! I had a short chat with the president, then immediately called Mom and Albert and half my friends, practically yelling into the phone: "The president just called me! The president just called me!" I'd met President Clinton once before, in '94 at the White House, when the Lady Tar Heels won the national championship. We got a group picture with him, and then each team member got an individual picture. Except that two of them didn't come out—Coop's and mine. I guess that night's phone call made up for the disappointment. Later on that same evening, I also got a call from the prime minister of Belize and one from Jesse Jackson. Little did I know at the time how short-lived my euphoria would be.

C.J. and I were asleep in bed when the phone rang again. It was 1:30 or 2 a.m., and I immediately thought something was wrong. And something was—but not anything I could have guessed. The voice was American and male: "There's been a report that your husband has tested positive for performance-enhancing drugs. Is he there? Can I get a comment?" Roused from sleep, I was completely befuddled. "W-what?" I think I said, and handed the phone to C.J., who frowned, his face tight and furious. "Don't call us here," he barked, and hung up. Obviously, we didn't sleep any more that night. C.J. made calls to everyone, trying to piece it together, trying to gauge what had happened. I don't remember what I did; I think I was in shock. It seemed so strange, so very strange.

The next morning all hell broke loose. Everyone had the story. It was on all the news reports and in all the papers: *C.J. Hunter tests positive*. I had no doubt that something was very wrong, that somehow C.J. had been set up. The timing was so peculiar—C.J. wasn't competing in these Olympics. He hadn't competed in months, ever since his knee problems started. And these purported tests were two months old. Apparently C.J. had failed not one, not two, but four tests. The substance in question was nandrolone, an anabolic steroid.

I could hardly believe this was happening. It was horrible. It was what every athlete has nightmares about, waking up with chills in the middle of the night. I just didn't get it. My family was staying across town, and they must have woken up, seen the news and wondered what the hell was going on. Sure enough, Mom and my uncle turned up at our apartment to see how I was doing. I explained the situation as best I could, but I didn't get it myself. "We know nothing about this whole thing," I told them. That's what C.J. had told me. He was as shocked as I was. I had no reason to disbelieve him.

My mom came through, of course—she always does when I don't know where to turn. She knew the attorney Johnnie Cochran, who had become something of a family friend, had quietly come to Sydney to watch me run the 100m. She put us in touch—I talked to him, and so did C.J. He didn't play a public role—and I don't believe he gave C.J. any kind of legal advice—but since he'd been the one to get me out of that terrible suspension when I had inadvertently missed a drug test in high school, it was comforting to have him around.

From then on, it was really C.J.'s gig. The first thing he did was to track down Victor Conte, who was in Sydney for the Games. C.J. and Victor Conte knew each other very well. His company is the now-infamous BALCO (Bay Area Laboratory Co-operative), and a sister company of Conte's, SNAC Systems, sold ZMA. ZMA was one of the supplements his laboratory made (the name ZMA is derived from the ingredients, which are zinc monomethionine aspartane, magnesium aspartane, and vitamin B-6), which was supposed to help you sleep better and to let your muscles regenerate and recover. Conte used to send C.J. supplements. I never thought twice about it because SNAC made supplements not just for athletes but also for the general public; at the time, I figured it must be legitimate. I bought (and still buy) my supplements from GNC, but if this company owner wanted to supply C.J. with his supplements for free, then great. I had no problem with it.

A press conference was arranged for the following day. C.J. left before me with Charlie, Trevor and Trevor's wife. He was already up on the podium with Conte when I arrived with my bodyguard, a Nike representative, and the Sydney police escort who'd been assigned to me for the duration of the Games. There was also a PR person from Nike who was helping us handle the press conference—C.J. was also a Nike athlete.

▲ When C.J. held a press conference to face the allegations of failing multiple drug tests, I felt it was necessary to be by his side and show my support for him.

◄ C.J.'s story—and mine, as his wife at the time—was big news for a few days and ended up on the cover of Sports Illustrated.

# ALL I COULD THINK WAS:

# I'VE GOT TO RUN.

## I'VE GOT TO RUN AND GET AWAY FROM THIS.

Beforehand, I'd weighed the pros and cons of making a statement, and decided that of course I'd stand up and say I believed my husband was innocent. Yes, I knew he was taking supplements, but I was also taking supplements. Every athlete out there takes supplements! I was taking the same ones I take now—vitamin E, vitamin C, a multivitamin, amino acids, calcium, flax seed oil, and glutamine—a significant list, but all generally available at any drugstore or health store. I take more than the average person because I'm an athlete and I train hard. I assumed that my husband was doing just the same, so why a test should show up positive was beyond me.

I wanted to stand up for C.J., but I did have misgivings. There were so many rumors flying around, and I actually wasn't as familiar with the whole situation as I could've been. I dreaded saying the wrong thing. On some level, I was also concerned about my focus being shifted from the task ahead of me, but there was no way around that problem now. I discussed my statement with the PR people and those running the press conference, and decided I was going to be brief and to the point. I wouldn't cry. I wouldn't turn this into an emotional circus. I would show my support for my husband and then would exit.

So in the middle of the press conference I got up and I made my statement: "I support my husband 100 percent. I believe he is innocent. . . ." Then I left the stage, got into the car and went home.

Alone in the apartment, I mulled over all the shreds of information I'd gleaned, trying to make sense of this senseless situation. Earlier that day, I'd heard C.J. and Victor and Trevor debating how nandrolone could have shown up in C.J.'s system. Was it a tainted supplement? Perhaps from some other company—not Conte's, naturally—that cleaned their machinery less than scrupulously? In the press conference, Conte put forth that theory. He'd also implied that the levels of nandrolone in C.J.'s tests were merely traces—far, far lower than the thousand times over the legal limit that had been reported of C.J.'s tests. There'd also been talk about the timing of the leak. It smelled fishy. Who had leaked the report to the press anyway? What had they gained by holding on to these alleged positive results until the Olympics?

That afternoon, my uncle and mom came over, and we hugged and sat down and talked it through. Was there some kind of conspiracy at work here? Since C.J. wasn't competing, was it me who was being targeted? Could it be that someone didn't want me to succeed? To this day I'm not sure I'm sold on the conspiracy theory, but my uncle and mom helped me to realize how it might be very useful to consider it. "Why not believe it?" they asked. "Use it as your fire, your motivation to continue. What if someone really is trying to get to you? Are you going to let them rattle you?" It was the same type of fuel I'd always used to give me an edge—only this was on a whole different scale. And I used it. Nobody but my family ever suspected that paranoia helped me to run faster in Sydney 2000.

In fact, it wasn't only the possibility of some saboteur trying to foil my attempt at an Olympic record that bugged me; it was the failure, again, of USA Track & Field to take any position at all. I understood why they didn't say anything on C.J.'s behalf—after all, he had tested positive, and that was indefensible. But I felt abandoned, too. Over the next couple of days, allegations flew back and forth. The International Olympic Committee accused the U.S. Olympic committee and USA Track & Field of knowing about C.J.'s positive tests and covering them up. And if the IAAF had administered the tests, why had they not released the results before now? This whole thing was degenerating into some America vs. the World scenario. So I kept away from it all. I stopped reading the papers and watching the news. I had e-mail and phone calls from so many friends expressing their support—and my family was by my side—but the silence from officials in my sport was loud; it was as if they were too nervous to approach me. It was also guilt by association all over again, like my temporary ban in high school for missing a test, like not speaking up for Florence Griffith Joyner after her death.

Two days after the press conference, I was back in competition for the first heats of the 200m and the qualifying rounds of the long jump. It was a relief to get to the track again after the tsunami of publicity, but I wasn't prepared for the new atmosphere I found there. It had soured, to say the least. It was normal for all eyes to be on me when I walked across the warm-up track, but this time I felt like the back of my head was being burned off. I had a feeling of deep shame. There was no reason I should feel that way. I couldn't fathom it, nor could I dismiss it; it felt like hell. I wouldn't wish that feeling on my worst enemy.

The 200m warm-up was the hardest of my life. All I could think was: *I've got to run. I've got to run and get away from this.* Then I ran the first round, no problem. The second felt effortless too—so much so that I slowed up toward the end . . . and the Australian favorite Melinda Gainsford-Taylor beat me to the tape. The crowd, of course, went wild. She and I both knew that this was an anomaly, but it made for a sweet moment. It released a little tension for me too—at least until the next event, the long jump. I had issues with the long jump of course, and my emotional state did nothing to improve my consistency. The whole time I was thinking: *I've just got to get through this. I've just got to get through this* . . . and I very nearly didn't. I managed to qualify only on my third jump—very close to not reaching the finals.

That day seemed to never end. In between the first two 100m heats, I'd gone back to the apartment. This time I stayed in the warm-up area for the two hours between the 200m heats, then went back to wait for the long jump. Though I don't socialize between heats, I would normally have spent some of that time with C.J. But C.J. wasn't there. He'd had his credentials removed. He could get into the stadium, but was no longer allowed in the warm-up area. In fact, I didn't even know where he was.

It was right that C.J. was banned from mingling with other athletes, because positive tests taint the sport. But I still thought he was innocent, even though he was being treated as guilty. Deep down I believed that he would be exonerated, that the black cloud would pass over and this whole thing would be revealed as a huge mistake. There have been a number of athletes in the history of track and field who tested positive but were later cleared. One of the most egregious examples was the British 800m runner, Diane Modahl, in 1994. She fought her ban in court—she practically went bankrupt paying lawyers and court fees but, when it did indeed turn out there had been a problem with the test, her name had been dragged through the mud and she'd lost valuable competitive years. From horror stories like that, I knew drug tests were far from infallible.

I got a quick massage after the long jump, then I think I went over to the apartment where my family was staying, and Mom cooked. Or maybe Trevor and Charlie came over and we ordered in. I honestly don't know. I barely remember that evening. I don't think I even saw C.J.—he was in and out the apartment the whole time, dealing with everything, talking to people. However, I remember sleeping well. I was utterly exhausted, more emotionally than physically, because I hadn't had to run all that fast yet.

The next day, Thursday, September 28, I awoke feeling brighter. I had the 200m semifinals and final to look forward to. Again, I barely saw C.J. that day. I spent a good part of it on e-mail, drinking about two gallons of water (nonstop hydration is a ritual of mine on race day, to cleanse myself of impurities). Eventually, after winning the semifinals, the final came. There had been cameras everywhere I went for the past two days, way more than usual. After warming up and stripping off, I wasn't surprised to find a camera peering up at me from behind my blocks when I walked up to the start line. If you want to know the one thing I remember about the 200m Olympic final, it was this. Just before "take your marks" I bent down, looked that cameraman right in the eye and whispered, "If you only knew how bad I have to pee."

▲ The long jump had always been a hit-or-miss
event for me—and that fact was never more
apparent than in Sydney when I took bronze.

I REMEMBER BEING CHOKED
WITH DISAPPOINTMENT. IT
WAS ONLY MY THIRD EVENT,
AND MY HOPES AND DREAMS
WERE ALREADY DASHED.

He collapsed laughing. And that made me laugh. The cameraman said, "Hey, all the more reason to get to the finish line faster," and we laughed some more. Right before the final. I remember getting into the blocks, and I don't know if I had a smile on my face, but I definitely had one in my head. I'd managed to displace all the mess of the past days with this ridiculous moment. I was proud of myself for that because it meant I was able to enjoy the race. Yes, sure, it wasn't the most comfortable 200 meters of my life, but I ran it in 21.84—0.45 seconds faster than Pauline Davis-Thompson, the silver medalist. Maybe the cameraman had been onto something.

I was happy all over again, and I was relieved—I could get to the bathroom now! Really, though, I was relieved it was over, that I'd gotten through it and I'd won. Not that I'd been in any doubt that I'd win the 200m, but it was still a relief. Then I was thinking one thing only: *Two down, three to go.*

But first I had to run the press gamut. There's a gentleman from the IAAF who for the past several years had been escorting athletes down what we call Interview Row, and that day he was my lifeline. At each stop, after I'd answered the first question, which was invariably, "How does it feel to win the 200m gold medal at the Olympics?" he'd say, "Sorry, but Marion has to move on." He got me through in record time. I've never thanked him properly for that. When I got to the press conference, the bronze and silver medalists took some of the heat off me; and the whole C.J. story had cooled—to some extent, anyway—and I wasn't too heavily grilled about it.

I was really excited about the long jump final the next day. I'd managed to put the uncertainties of the qualifying round out of my mind, convincing myself that I'd just had an off day. But again, to my dismay, the competition started out badly. My steps just weren't together. I felt unsure on the runway because I didn't know what to expect once I got to the board or what to expect in the air. It was plain that when Heike stepped on the runway, or Montavo from Spain or the Greek athletes, they weren't dogged by the same uncertainty. My eyes, which had been shut tight when I'd started competing in the long jump, were slowly starting to open, and the truth was beginning to penetrate my insane loyalty: Trevor hadn't taught me right. I shouldn't be trusting luck in the Olympic final. I should know how to hit the board every time.

I really don't know which jump it was that got me the bronze. I know my last jump was a foul. It was extremely long and close enough that I had to have the official point out my mark to me, but it didn't count. I had failed in my bid for five gold medals.

Heike won, and I remember hugging her, congratulating her and lining up behind her and Fiona May of Italy and walking off the field waving to the crowd. And I also remember being choked with disappointment. It was only my third event, and my hopes and dreams were already dashed.

I hadn't been prepared. Obviously I was fast enough—I had two gold medals to prove that my fitness wasn't the problem. I just wasn't ready. Leaving the stadium that night, there was a deathly silence in the van. When he got in, Trevor slammed his fist on the seats. "This is my fault!" he said through gritted teeth. *You're damn right this is your fault,* I was thinking. *Everyone's been telling you my technique is horrible, but I trusted that you knew what you were doing.* I was boiling in the backseat. My hopes were up so high for those five golds, and there was no way I could have made it. I mean, I might've had a lucky break in the long jump, but it shouldn't have come to that. I should have been more prepared. I was pissed with myself for not seeing it sooner and felt foolish about my bold pronouncement. But most of all, I was furious with Trevor. When we got to my apartment, I didn't even say good night. I resolved then and there to make some changes—exactly what, I wasn't yet sure. But the next time I jumped, I swore I'd know what I was doing. As it turned out, I didn't jump again for three and a half years.

My disappointment carried into that night. C.J. was back, but I barely remember his presence. My uncle and mom had helped me understand that I shouldn't focus on him then. I couldn't do anything to help what was happening with him. All I could control were my performances in these Olympic Games. Both of my relays—where I could impact only one-fourth of the result—were up next, and they were going to take place on the same day.

The day after the long jump, a 4x100m team practice was scheduled. Nanceen Perry, a young 200m specialist from the University of Texas, was going to run Inger's third leg. Because she was inexperienced in handing off to me, we'd have more of a challenge ahead, but we were still totally optimistic. However, I was beginning to feel fatigued. For six long days I'd been warming up, competing, warming up, competing. And I'd been assaulted by so many emotions. And even with Inger missing, our team chemistry for the 4x100m was weak. Nanceen, a younger girl who'd been thrown into this at the last minute, was running third. Gail Devers's second leg was taken by the inexperienced Torri Edwards, an up-and-coming sprinter at the time. And leading off was Chryste Gaines, never my favorite because she had nothing positive to say about her fellow athletes, but since she'd been around so long, people listened to her. It was not good for the sport.

Warming up for the final, we smiled as we stretched together, which felt really fake. We said our prayer, which always seems scripted to me, but I did it for the team. Getting hyped up for this relay felt like a chore, but we were all out there because we wanted to do well for our country. So I was as focused as ever.

My training teammate, Chandra Sturrup, was on the track, running for the Bahamas. We'd always play a game in practice in which the Bahamian team would beat the U.S. team in the finals of the 4x100m—sort of as a ongoing gag. Or so I always thought. But when Chryste ran a slow first leg and the Bahamian team got a great start, I wasn't laughing so hard. Torri ran very well for the position she was put in, though the handoff to Nanceen was clumsy. Considering that neither the curve nor the 100m was her specialty, I thought Nanceen did fine, but by the time I got the baton after another botched pass, I was 15 meters behind the pack. I managed to make up some of that, but not enough. Chandra's Bahamian team got the gold. We got bronze.

For the amount of practice we had, our finish was a small miracle, but the disappointment for me was harsh. I was thinking, *This could be really bad.* Luckily, I didn't have to deal with the media or go to the medal stand, because I was due back at the track immediately for the 4x400m final. (I'd been excused the early heats because of all my other events.) It was my last event. Walking back to the warm-up track in the fading evening light, something seemed different. It took me a while to figure out what it was: I was alone. No bodyguards, no police escorts, no other athletes. It was almost the only time throughout the entire Games that I'd been by myself. Normally I'd have relished it, but I wasn't peaceful. I was disappointed. I was heading over to join a team I loved, but in a distance that was hardly my specialty. I was worried. I was tired.

When I got over there, I found my teammates debating whether to put me in the anchor spot. Luckily, with these girls, everything was open and genuine. "Okay," I said. "If you really want me to run anchor and nobody else steps up, I'll do it. But let me tell you, I've been running for days. I'm exhausted. I can give you a good 200 meters, but after that I have no idea how my body will respond."

▲ We fell short in the 4x100m relay, winning bronze for Team USA. After the race, my relay teammate, Nanceen Perry, and I caught our breath.

◀ *(previous page, from left to right:) LaTasha Colander-Richardson, Monique Hennagan (my old track teammate from UNC), me and Jearl Miles Clark celebrate after winning gold for Team USA in the 4x400m relay.*

▲ *(top left) Before the start of the 4x400m relay, I wasn't sure how much energy I had left in my legs but was determined to give the race everything I had.*

▲ *(top right) After I got the baton in the 4x400m relay, I ended up running a strong leg and helping Team USA to win gold.*

▲ *After winning my fifth medal, I didn't realize right away that I'd made history as the first woman to win five track and field medals in a single Olympic Games.*

We decided I'd run the third leg. One of the veterans of the team, Jearl Miles Clark, had come down with something and wasn't feeling well, but she would still run first. Second leg was my former Carolina track teammate, Monique Hennagan, and anchor would be LaTasha Colander-Richardson. With this as my last event, I knew all eyes were on me, yet I hadn't run a 4x400m since college. I was nervous. "Marion, you're gonna do great," said Jearl—a real sweetheart. "It's the last one. We'll win this gold. You're going to leave these Games and you're still going to make history. We promise you that."

Well, Jearl, especially for a sick person, ran great, and Monique also ran a very good second leg, then I got the baton. I felt fine, but that was no surprise for the first 200 meters. Then I got to 250 meters and I was still feeling great. I had energy; I had more to give—300, and I still had turnover. *What is going on here?* I wondered, grinning to myself. At 350 meters, I was still steaming ahead. I was jubilant. Maybe I hit the wall in the last 10 meters, but any 400m runner would pay good money to hit it that late. After I handed the baton to LaTasha, I wasn't even drop-dead tired. It was almost a miracle. I guess I got us a good lead, which LaTasha was able to hold, and that was it. We'd done it. We'd won.

We all took off for a victory lap (which I was doubtful I'd be able to complete!) and Jearl was skipping along, saying, "See! I told you. I told you we'd do it!" This may sound naive, but it was only at that moment that it truly came home to me for the first time: Running a relay is a *team* effort. My goal of five golds had involved all the ladies of the four-by-one, plus all these women of the four-by-four. I honestly hadn't seen it that way before. In that sense, I'd been selfish in thinking I was going to win five when it had never been all up to me. I turned to Jearl and beamed at her.

"You're right," I said. "We did make history, didn't we?"

It was only later on at the press conference that I understood exactly what Jearl had meant. It wasn't just that our team had won this particular event in this Olympics. It was bigger than that. When a reporter asked me, "How does it feel to be the only woman ever to win five medals at a single Olympics?" I did a double take. "Wait a minute." I said. "Let me think about that. You mean. . . ." People had always talked about the five *golds*; nobody had mentioned to me that no woman had ever won five track and field *medals* in a single Olympic Games. I'd made history after all, and I hadn't even known it.

I can't pretend that this made everything okay, but I definitely felt a bit better. That night I celebrated with my family at their apartment. My Mom cooked and my little cousins wore my medals, and we had a great time. C.J. didn't come. Mom still hadn't voiced her misgivings about C.J., but I didn't want to make her feel awkward. It didn't seem like the right thing for him to celebrate with us, not after what had happened. I was sure my mom felt her daughter would have had the most perfect Olympic Games if it hadn't been for him. Again, she didn't say it in so many words, but I thought it was appropriate to leave him out of this party. C.J., who was happy for me despite his problems, must have understood because he didn't bring it up.

We—my family and I without C.J.—tried to do some sightseeing over the next couple of days, but it was a disaster. I couldn't go anywhere without causing chaos. Why I thought I'd be able to roam unnoticed, I'm not sure. Partly because of that, but mostly because our scheduled departure time was leaked to the press, which would have made our flight out of Kingsford-Smith a media circus, C.J. and I ended up leaving Sydney early. We hadn't planned on going to the closing ceremonies anyway, so suddenly we found ourselves at the airport taking an evening flight home. It felt like running away. Even though I had no reason to be ashamed or uncomfortable, I felt exposed. People always look at me, but the way I was being stared at as I left the Olympic city felt like the wrong kind of attention. I hadn't broken any laws, I'd only broken a record. But I felt like a fugitive.

# LOSSES

8.

For two months after Sydney, I flung myself into a post-Olympics media tour. I traveled abroad and all over the U.S., doing TV shows all over Europe, photo shoots, and various things for TAG, my watch company, and for Nike. I was on Letterman and Leno and Regis's show, and on Rosie O'Donnell. My PR team did a great job of keeping everyone "on message," so I talked mostly about my successes in Sydney and only had to answer a few questions about C.J. I thoroughly enjoyed it all, but it was also a lot of work. When I was a child I dreamed of having my name in the papers, of being on the talk shows, of having my own shoe. And I got it all—plus a whole lot more. And I am over the moon about that. Yet I tend to tell kids starting out in the sport, be careful what you wish for . . . because there is a downside. Fame comes with baggage.

The deterioration of my marriage was not a direct result of my realizing my dream, of course. But Sydney had left us with a gaping hole in our communication, which my media tour hardly helped to heal. In 1999, I had invested in some land in Chapel Hill—the first thing I'd ever bought for myself with my earnings—and I'd started designing a dream house. At the time, though, we were still living in a house in nearby Apex. But I hardly saw it. I hardly saw C.J. The cracks in our relationship that appeared in Berlin and widened in Sydney continued to grow. Even when I was home, we didn't talk much. I tried to open discussions with C.J. about his drug tests, but I always got the same dusty

answers: "I don't know how it happened—I wasn't taking anything," he'd say. And then he'd add, "But we're going to fight it." He also told me he was planning to retire, anyway, and wouldn't have to deal with it anymore. The whole business was sounding more and more suspicious to me. I could see how one test, even two tests, could have gone wrong—but four separate tests had came back positive. And the levels had been so incredibly high. How could he not have known *something*?

Worse still, with C.J. out of the public eye, it was only me being constantly asked about him. All I could do was keep proclaiming my husband's innocence, parroting his vague statements: "We don't know what happened" and "We're going to fight this." After a while, I started to wonder, *What exactly is it that we're fighting? And why?*

By Thanksgiving, all the interviews were over and I came back down to earth. We spent the holiday same as we always had: I went to Mom's place to celebrate alone with her, then later, C.J.'s mom cooked dinner at our place for us, C.J.'s ex-wife and their kids, Corey and Ahny. C.J. and his ex-wife had their issues, which I stayed out of, but she was always fine with me. She lived down the street (I had helped C.J. buy the house), so we saw a lot of them, and I had a good rapport with the kids, who called me Marion. But Thanksgiving wasn't very joyful that year. All I wanted was to get back to training.

I started on the first of December. After the highs of the 2000 season, my body still needed to recuperate some, so I began extremely slowly. Which meant I had plenty of time to brood about my marriage.

All that December, C.J. and I alternated between stony silences and stupid squabbles, not seeing eye to eye. We had progressively less contact, almost just passing each other in the hall. I felt like a prisoner in my own home, stalked by the unaccountable shame I'd been feeling since Sydney. It bothered me that C.J. never apologized for his part in causing me extra pressure at the Olympics, or even asked me what I'd been through there and how I'd felt about it all. And as I said earlier, his spiky personality annoyed me more and more. Though he never lost his temper with me, he was capable of the most disgusting manners toward strangers. At the end of a flight, for example, if someone knocked into him slightly while getting their bag, he'd explode at them: *What you do that for?* He had a short fuse, and I was sick of it. I began to think the "Beauty and the Beast" line that so many papers used to describe us might be apt after all. I wasn't necessarily the Beauty, but C.J. sure played the Beast at times. The funny, caring, protective guy whose company I so enjoyed was nowhere in sight.

Not long after the New Year, I realized I didn't want to be with him anymore and decided to leave. I worried that I was rushing into it, that I should take longer to mull it over, but it was clear enough. I simply didn't have any warm feelings left in my heart for C.J. Perhaps he'd killed my trust in Sydney, or even before that. Perhaps I'd simply outgrown the relationship.

Without telling anyone, not even my mom, I found an apartment in Morrisville, the next town over from Apex. I told C.J. our marriage wasn't working any more and I was going to move out. "You won't do it," he said. I told him I'd already found an apartment, to which he responded, "Okay, move out, but we can still try to make it work." *Make what work?* I thought. Then the next day, he would get upset and yell, "Go ahead then! Move out!" I was just tired of it, sick of the whole thing. One day, when C.J. was at work—he was then a strength and conditioning coach for the North Carolina State football team—I had my stuff moved into my new apartment and my furniture put in storage. I asked Johnnie Cochran to recommend a local divorce attorney, told C.J. he could live in the house and started my new life.

It was, not surprisingly, a difficult winter. It had its bright spots. The lows, however, were pretty dire. But a trip to Belize early in January for a huge celebration in my honor was a welcome journey. Mom came, of course, and we visited with my uncle there. I was given the key to Belize City, I was made the country's ambassador of sports, and the national stadium was renamed after me. It was a tremendous honor and I loved every minute of it. It was wonderful that my Belizean heritage was acknowledged in that way. It really meant a lot to me.

In January, I received the Jesse Owens International Trophy, an honor that made an indelible impression on me. U.S. Track & Field gives an annual Jesse Owens award (I was fortunate enough to receive it twice before, in 1997 and 1998; I would also win it again in 2002), but this one had a broader focus. The award was given to someone who helped promote better understanding between nations. Jesse Owens himself had not enjoyed that opportunity. He won an unprecedented four gold medals at the 1936 Berlin Olympics (in an atmosphere of antiblack Nazi propaganda) but was never congratulated by the president, Franklin Delano Roosevelt. In the same year, an equivalent general athletic award was given to the white decathlete who won only a single gold. In 1935, when Owens had set six world records—including three in one day—the award had gone to a white golfer. Back home after his dazzling Olympic feats, Jesse Owens had to run races against horses and motorcycles to make a living. I'd always believed it was a deep disgrace that he wasn't recognized as a hero while he was still in his prime, and I'm glad to see how far we've progressed since then. I'd always thought, if I could made a fraction of Owens's impact on the track, I could do some good for my sport. But I hadn't grasped the effect I could have on people around the world, how what I do touches people's lives. I was surprised and delighted to be singled out as somebody who can make a difference.

THE FUNNY, CARING,
PROTECTIVE GUY WHOSE
COMPANY I SO ENJOYED
WAS NOWHERE IN SIGHT.

▲ I'd always thought, if I could make a fraction of
Owens's impact on the track, I could do some
good for my sport.

The big awards made for a stark contrast with my life at home. It was downright quiet. I was settling into my new routine, going to practice every day, seeing a lot of my mom, and talking and e-mailing with my friends, who were supporting me 100 percent. In fact, I was really starting to enjoy it. For the first time ever, I was living on my own. I had my dog, was paying my own bills and doing my own thing. I was extremely independent, and I liked it. What wasn't so great was seeing C.J. every day. Since he was based at N.C. State and I was back at the track with Trevor, we couldn't avoid meeting in the weight room. Those were some chilly moments. But we became cordial after not too long, then progressed to pleasant. After things settled down between us, we agreed it was time to tell Trevor what was going on with us. We sat him down and explained how he'd played such a big part in our relationship, and how we thought he should know we'd separated and were getting a divorce. I don't think he was too surprised. He said he hoped both of our individual relationships with him would continue as before. I didn't see a problem with that, though things between Trevor and me would start to suffer soon enough.

Late in January, I was at home one afternoon, when Trevor called. "Marion, are you sitting down?" He sounded deadly serious. "What are you talking about, Trevor?" I thought he was in his jokester mode. It happened a lot.

"I just got a call from Charlie. . . ."

"Oh, yes, he left me a message too. I was about to call him back."

"Listen. I wanted to tell you face to face, but you need to know right now." I went icy cold. What was going on? I could hear Trevor take a deep breath. "Your father has passed away."

I sat down. I had no idea what to say or feel. It was completely out of the blue. I hadn't thought about my father in so long. I hadn't seen him in I didn't know how many years. I turned down Trevor's offer of help, hung up and just sat there, memories flashing through my mind. The abortive laundromat visits. His apparition at my Lady Tar Heels game against Stanford. His ignoring my letters, my birthdays. Me.

I called Charlie for the whole story. He told me that someone from my father's church somehow knew he had this famous daughter and had found me on the Internet and called my management company, Vector Sports. The Jones family hadn't called. If it weren't for this kind lady—not even a close friend of my father's—I'd have had no idea my own father had died.

I called the lady, who didn't know much but who gave me the number of my father's girlfriend, Kathy Miles. Kathy Miles . . . it sounded familiar. Could I possibly have met her when I was a child? I dialed her number, and she finally answered. She was in a state. She started bawling right away. "Is this really Marion? Is this really Marion?" she kept asking between sobs. I assured her it was, and that I was hoping for some more details. I also offered to help with the funeral. She could barely speak from grief. She managed to tell me that he'd died only yesterday but was too hysterical to explain what had happened. Then she gave me the number of my father's brother, who was taking care of the arrangements.

I called my father's brother, Uncle Edward. I thought I might have met him once, but I wasn't sure. He was already planning the funeral, so I started to talk details with him, but all the time I was thinking, *You knew your brother had a daughter. And you never thought of making one phone call?* He assured me he didn't need any help, but I'd already decided. I was going to fly out to California. I would meet my family (that was a tough concept), take care of whatever business needed attention and say goodbye to my father, whom I barely knew.

When I told Mom, she was just as shocked as I'd been. She cried. She had long since cut all emotional ties with her second husband, but she knew how I must be feeling. She was crying more for me, I think. When she offered to come to California, I almost said yes, then thought better of it. I didn't know the situation with this girlfriend, and I had no idea how big the family was or what they were like. Mom shouldn't have to deal with any of this; it was my story now. Charlie Wells did come with me, though, and just in case of anything, we brought the Vector Sports security guard who accompanied us to meets in the U.S.

As soon as we landed in L.A., I headed for Kathy Miles's place, alone. It was a house my father owned next door to his laundromat—a house I'd been past a million times without a clue it was his. She answered the door, still tear-stained and distraught, but very welcoming. "Kathy," I said, trying to calm her down. "I'm here because I need information. About what happened. Some background on my father. Anything." Then she brought out a large scrapbook stuffed full and opened it up on the coffee table. It was crammed with newspaper and magazine articles about me, from my high school days up to and including the Olympics. Everything I'd sent him from Carolina—all the basketball memorabilia, the notes and photographs—was glued in place. He'd been following my career as carefully as any serious fan. Kathy said he used to take this around to his friends' houses and proudly show them clippings about me. "You see," she said. "He *was* keeping up with you!"

After Kathy calmed down, she told me some other things about my father. "We were never married, but he was like my husband," she said. She kept repeating that phrase: "He was like my husband." The Jones family, she said, wanted to keep her away from the funeral and she didn't know what to do. They'd been together for years, she explained. It turned out I had probably met her at some point, since she was already seeing my father before he'd married my mother and during their marriage, too. Maybe she had come by his laundromat one time when I was little and stayed with my father. I couldn't pinpoint the moment, but I knew we'd met.

As for how he'd died, it seemed that one day the week before at the laundromat, my father wasn't feeling well, so he went next door to Kathy's place—his house—to rest. Kathy said he never took time off work for any reason, so, worried, she drove him home. The same thing happened the next day, and when she dropped him off, she asked him if he wanted her to stay. He said no, he was fine. When he didn't answer his phone all night, Kathy became worried and went over with one of her sons (not by my father) the next day. They found him dead in the bathroom. He must have had a heart attack or a stroke and fallen and knocked his head. They called the police, Uncle Edward and my father's sisters. No autopsy was done.

Kathy gave me keys to my father's house, and the following day I went over there. My father was always very neat, but the place was a mess; there was stuff everywhere. Furniture was overturned, ornaments were broken, the mattress had been dragged off the bed. It looked like somebody had robbed the place—or maybe somebody had been in there searching for something. Then Uncle Edward showed up. He gave me an awkward, fake hug. The first thing out of his mouth was, "We didn't find a will." He made it sound like, "That's what you're here for isn't it?" "*What?*" I said. "I just wanted to see my father's house, to learn something about him. I didn't even think about any will." "Well, we didn't find it," he said. The whole thing stunk. I decided I'd better find an attorney in the area who dealt with estates, in case something got out of hand.

▲ I was on my own during the 2001 season after separating from C.J. at the beginning of the year. In July 2001, I was at the Norwich Union Grand Prix in England.

▶ In February 2001, I won an ESPY award for the 2000 Female Athlete of the Year.

SEVERAL YOUNG
PEOPLE ABOUT MY
AGE ALL GOT UP
WITH TEARS
STREAMING DOWN
THEIR FACES AND
SAID HE WAS LIKE
A FATHER TO THEM.
THAT WAS THE
HARDEST PART.

The funeral was weird. I sat in the front row with the family—and watched one person after another stand up to eulogize my father. The pastor asked me if I wanted to say something, but I declined. What did I have to say? Nothing positive, really nothing much at all. I didn't know the man. Even so, I was crying. I was crying *because* I didn't know him. Among the speakers were several young people about my age who all got up with tears streaming down their faces and said he was like a father to them. That was the hardest part.

After an agonizing hour and a half, we all went to the cemetery. He was being buried in a mausoleum, and there was another ceremony. Again, as kin, I sat in the front row surrounded by the Jones family. All the mourners trooped past to pay their respect. All these nieces and nephews and cousins I'd never met, and friends of my father's who knew him so much better than I did were shaking my hand and offering their sympathies. And at the same time, they'd all whisper excitedly how they'd been watching me and following my successes. It was surreal. It would have been almost funny if it wasn't so sad.

The wake at Uncle Edward's was no less awkward. He said all the family really wanted to meet me, and, indeed, my father's sisters—my aunts—introduced themselves and gave me warm, genuine hugs. I was keeping an eye out for someone I remembered meeting as a small child, someone who was introduced as my older brother. When I'd asked Mom about that, she'd said yes, she remembered my father mentioning he had a son. But he wasn't there. I felt so out of place with all these strangers who were family that I'd never met. I couldn't wait to leave.

The next day I stopped off at my father's house before going to the attorney, to gather any documents—birth certificate, driver's license, anything. I knew he was born in Louisiana, but that was all. I was even fuzzy on the date. Still, I couldn't find enough to be able to answer the attorney's questions, especially about this supposed son, so I had the lawyer call Uncle Edward. That's when things got iffy. He refused to talk and passed her on to his sister, my aunt, who also remembered some vague story about a son. Obviously a son, as next of kin, would be entitled to the estate.

To this day, the process is continuing. We hired a private investigator, but no son was found, so I was named administrator of the estate. I had the attorney embark on dividing the estate appropriately, while I took a backseat. I'd never thought about it before, but now that I was involved, it struck me that my mother should get something. All those years of struggling alone without any child support certainly entitled her to some of her ex-husband's assets. Kathy Miles also hired an attorney to make a claim as the common-law wife. Then another woman turned up saying she was married to my father and that he'd signed over the deeds of his properties to her. She produced a marriage document. The problem was, the document said she was married to my father at the same time as my mother. Then, when I visited my father's house in March (before Mt. SAC) just to check on it, I found that the whole place had been stripped. The only person with a key was Uncle Edward—and Kathy Miles, who'd given her key to me, and I was sure it wasn't her. The whole thing just got messier and messier. In the end (in 2004), rather than pour money into investigations that would only turn up information I didn't want to know about, I cut my losses and decided just to take a chunk of the estate for my mother and split the rest between Kathy Miles and this woman, his other wife.

All that mess and intrigue about my father's estate couldn't distract me from the most unnerving discovery of all. If he was proud enough of me to keep everything I'd sent him, and to find and keep all of those clippings on me, and if he knew I was trying to contact him, then why did he avoid me? It was worse—

or more confusing at least—now that I'd found out he did care, yet still kept away. Back home after the funeral, I turned it over and over in my mind. Maybe he was reluctant to get in touch after I was successful because he'd come off as only interested in my fame or money. So, I asked myself: What would I have done if he contacted me last year? Would I have thought, hah, he's only calling because I'm on TV? No. I'm quite sure I'd have accepted him back into my life. Or perhaps he felt guilty and ashamed about the years of neglect? But then, he'd have avoided mentioning me to his friends, rather than boasting to them. Eventually, I had to accept that there were no answers. My father, George Jones, was a part of me. I'd kept his name. Perhaps I had his genes to thank for my speed. But I'd never understand him.

My new single life was going well, which helped ease things about my father's death. I was enjoying practice. I had my friends, especially Melissa and Tiffany, as confidantes. I saw a lot of Mom. My fury at Trevor over the long jump had cooled a bit. He told me he had consulted with some top long jump coach in Europe during the off-season. But it made no difference—I stuck to my decision about giving the long jump a rest in 2001. I said I was enjoying my training, and that's the truth: I love to work hard, and Chandra was there, which made it more fun—but things were not ideal with my coach.

Trevor and I no longer had an interpreter, which was a major change. C.J. had brought us together and had always been the intermediary for Trevor and me to talk business. After C.J. and I split, Trevor seemed unable to bring up business with me directly. Then, coming back after the Olympics, he wanted to renegotiate his contract. Which was fine by me, except that he proposed such an outrageous number—at least double his previous salary. It was out of the question. In addition to the long jump trouble, he'd increased the size of the group to about 17 or 18 athletes by then. Not only did he want more money from me, but he also got paid by many of them. Still others were getting free training, and he was also coaching football on the side.

Trevor was always the type to put his neck on the line for an athlete he trains. In that regard, he's very giving and caring. But if you're operating a business and have athletes who need—and pay for—your time, you can't be too charitable. At the time, he was probably getting paid more than any other coach in the world, yet he wanted more. We came to a financial agreement—not as much as he wanted, but more than before. But from then on, whenever we needed to negotiate, he would shy away, saying, "I'll get back to you" or "It's not a good time now" or some such excuse. I kept trying, even wrote letters, but to no avail. So after the beginning of 2001, I had my lawyer talk to him whenever we had business to discuss. I felt I had no choice, but it did nothing to help our communication.

One major problem I tried to discuss with him was his habit of bringing people into the group without telling me and without knowing their backgrounds. At this point in my career especially, I needed to know everything because if one of his athletes tested positive, *I* would be answering questions about it in a press conference, not Trevor. In fact, I found out much later that doping was exactly what had happened to various athletes Trevor had briefly taken under his wing in Raleigh, who then somehow disappeared from the sport.

Another thing suddenly missing from the mix was our shared attitude about how I competed. Before the Games, we'd had a similar "go get 'em" drive, a zest to prove wrong everybody who doubted me. But since Sydney, Trevor had lost that motivation and the passion that went with it. Even so, when the season finally started, with Mt. SAC, it went fine. It was very strange at first, because I had not been on the circuit alone before. I'd always had C.J. and a whole team. I really learned to be self-reliant then, to take my stack of DVDs and books and spend a lot of time in my hotel room. Dealing with being away from friends and family made me realize that all the other athletes had been doing it like that for years. It was quite an eye-opener.

▲ Zhanna Pintusevich-Block was the better sprinter during the 100m final at the IAAF World Championships in Edmonton, Canada. After the race, she let out some emotion on the track.

I competed a lot in 2001, as usual, and ran well—not nearly my fastest, but well enough to win—and the season sped past. In no time flat, it was August and time for the World Championships, which took place in Edmonton, Canada. It was true Trevor lacked passion that season, but I must admit I was also not firing on all cylinders. I trained my heart out, ran my very best in competitions, but never quite hit my stride in 2001. It wasn't until Edmonton that it all caught up with me. My first two rounds of the 100m were very good, but in my semifinal, Zhanna Pintusevich-Block outran me. When she passed me I couldn't switch up to a higher gear. It felt unreal. This simply never happened to me. I hadn't lost a 100m race since 1997. The walk back to the warm-up area was a long one. Trevor didn't say a word before the final; I warmed up in silence. Then I went back out there and it happened again. She beat me.

I had no excuses for the loss. At the press conference I told the reporters that today just wasn't my day, that Zhanna ran great and I applauded her. Again, I don't remember Trevor having anything to say. Then I won the 200m—it was one of the slowest World Championship–winning 200m performances in ages, but I was happy to have won. I have no recollection of running anchor in the 4x100m, which we won; I only remember leaving Edmonton under a black cloud of gloom. My season was pretty much over.

Trevor may not have said anything to me about the loss and the season in general, but I soon learned he was more forthcoming with others. Over the next few weeks, disturbing reports kept filtering back to me. Trevor had told various people that I got beaten because I hadn't trained as hard this year. Twice he told reporters that I didn't run so well in 2001 because I had so much going on in my personal life. That part I couldn't really argue with—I'd made the announcement in June that C.J. and I had separated—though I didn't think it was very professional of him to bring it up. But as for me not training hard—*that* infuriated me. I always, always, always train hard. Anyone who knows me knows that—and certainly Trevor knows that. I would never bring anything but full effort on the track, not even on Thanksgiving and Christmas Day. For years, Trevor had been party to my little quirk of training when the whole world has a day off—a psychological trick I play on myself to gain an edge. He'd often commented on that, on how I worked harder than any other athlete he knew. And now he was saying the opposite behind my back?

I felt slightly betrayed. With every statement coming from him, our once-solid relationship was crumbling. One of the people I trusted most in the sport was not on my side anymore. (In fact, two of them, because C.J. had also been integral to my running life.) I toyed with the idea of leaving Trevor, but he and I had so much history by then, and it's such a big deal in this sport for a top athlete to switch coaches. And who would I have gone to anyway? I did feel Trevor had let me down in 2001, since I'd trained just as hard as I had in the past. Then again, I told myself, maybe I'd just had an off year coming down from the Olympics. Or it could be that *we* had a down year as a team. It happens sometimes. Okay, I told myself, I did have a lot going on this year. I had some losses, a lot of distractions to deal with. I'll give him another chance.

◀ *I quickly put my loss at the World Championships behind me, winning the 100m in August 2001 at a Golden League meet in Zurich, Switzerland.*

**9**

**FASTEST COUPLE WORLD"**

◄ (previous page) Tim and I both won the 100m
at the 2002 Grand Prix Final in Paris. But Tim's
win was a defining moment: He set the current
100m world record of 9.78 seconds.

▲ Tim and I went to Hawaii at the end of the season
in 2002. It was our first vacation together.

I continued to run well throughout the 2002 season, but not as well as I'd hoped, after what turned out to be a good start. My performances were good enough to win—at Brussels, Monaco, Zurich, Paris, Rome, London, Oslo, Berlin, the U.S. Nationals, the World Cup, you name it. In fact, ironically, 2002 ended up being my first undefeated season. But I wasn't happy with my times. Who knows how much of it was connected to my rapport with Trevor gradually dissolving and our communications becoming increasingly tense.

I've known Tim Montgomery since 1997. He's an elite sprinter on the circuit and a fellow American. Tim was always at my landmark meets—from Indiana and Athens in 1997 to Sydney in 2000—competing in his event, the 100m. Then, just before the Olympics, he moved to Raleigh from Virginia to train with Trevor. Even then we hardly spoke. He was, after all, one of 20-odd sprinters Trevor was coaching—training sessions were still crowded affairs. More to the point, Trevor had warned me against him. He told me confidentially that Tim was a wild, wild guy, and a womanizer. *If he's such a liability, why did you bring him into the group?* I thought. But I trusted Trevor, so I figured, okay, let me stay away from him. This was not hard to do since Trevor also implied that Tim wasn't my biggest fan.

In fall 2001, Trevor's enforced month off was especially unwelcome. I had way too much time to reflect on my loss in the 100m at the worlds. I couldn't wait to get back on the track and train, train, train. Once I started, I found that yet again, Trevor had not sought out any long jump experts to get the information he needed. So I decided to take another year off from the event to concentrate on getting my sprints back to where they had been. I was happy with things at the beginning of the training season; I was running fast, and there were no business negotiations, since Trevor still seemed happy with the arrangement we'd settled on in 2001.

The tide truly started to turn between Trevor and me when Tim and I had our first heart-to-heart chat in July 2002. The team was flying to Rome when Tim and I got seated together for the first time ever. We hit it off immediately. Naturally, given the warnings I'd had, I was surprised at how well we got along. It didn't take long to find out that our coach had been no less forthcoming in telling Tim what *I* thought of *him*. Trevor had warned him to stay away from me because I didn't want anyone else in the group. (I'd find out later that he hadn't stopped with that.) That first revelation was quite the icebreaker, and I guess we were laughing and looking conspiratorial when, glancing back, I noticed Trevor was sitting just two rows behind us. I turned to Tim and said, "You know, your coach back there doesn't like the fact that we're up here talking." We both turned around, and there was Trevor with a face like thunder. It was hilarious. "You're right," Tim said. "He's not happy at all." So we started chatting about exactly why Trevor would want to prevent us from talking, even casually. It quickly became clear that the bad reviews of Tim that Trevor had been feeding me were nothing compared with the trashing I'd been taking. Apparently, I was an emotional liability, Trevor said. I was vulnerable and dangerous. I could get Tim kicked out the group in a flash. I'd smile at him to his face one minute, then stab him in the back the next. One detail that particularly hurt was finding out how Trevor would complain to Tim after every holiday, how that #!&*! Marion had once again "made him" go out there on Thanksgiving and Christmas. And all along that had been our little bonding ritual, our way of getting one up on the competition. He'd never said a word to me about resenting it. Trevor kept confiding this stuff to Tim, until Tim tired of it and stopped listening. No wonder Trevor wanted to keep us apart.

We got to Rome with about six days to spare before the race, so we had a lot of time to kill. It was the usual story of my being pretty much hotel-bound—to keep off my feet and preserve my leg strength, and to avoid the hassle of going everywhere with bodyguards because of the avid European fans. Also, I don't speak Italian. Expecting this, I'd brought my usual books and laptop and DVDs. I barely glanced at them. Tim and I just kept talking. We met in the hotel corridor—literally. We weren't saying anything intimate, but still, people love to spread rumors on the circuit, so we thought it best to meet in public. Tim would sit on the carpet by his door, I would sit by mine down the hall, and we'd talk like that for hours on end. One day, we heard a door open and caught Trevor peeking his head out, checking whether we were still there. It's funny, we didn't discuss this meeting tactic, and now I'm not sure why we thought it was so taboo to be seen together. I was single, after all, and so was Tim. I guess we both figured that we could live without the pressure of gossip. So, sitting yards apart on the floor in a Roman hotel, we clicked. We talked about training and running and home and friends and our dreams and aspirations, how fast we thought we could run. We also discovered that our family situations could hardly have been more different. My family, of course, is tiny and pretty reserved. We're outspoken, but we keep our deepest feelings to ourselves. On the other hand, Tim claimed his family could fill a soccer field—and they were upfront, effusive types.

One day the group was invited to a horse race in a small city outside Rome. At dinner afterward, I was doing the politically correct thing, sitting with our host, when suddenly Tim got up and stormed away from the table. Later, he told me what had happened. Trevor, obviously terrified of our getting to know each other, had jokingly but seriously told Tim he'd just written himself a "one-way ticket out of the group." It's odd, but I believe Trevor hoped I'd never get to hear about what he did. He certainly never said a word to me about how the new friendship between Tim and me bothered him. After this little incident, though, Tim felt no further need to pretend to the group that we were still strangers.

Tim and I both knew we'd be meeting up when we got home to Raleigh. The first time we went out it was for dinner and a movie—which sounds like a date, but it was more casual than that. Soon, we started spending more time with each other. We'd go out or watch movies at home and cook for each other. In fact, we saw each other almost every day. We'd never looked twice at each other in *that* way before, but once I got to know Tim better, and learned a bit about how his mind works, how he expresses himself, that changed. I don't think many people have a real measure of Tim Montgomery. He's complex and he covers up his depths, puts up a front so it looks like he takes everything lightly. But he's a deep thinker. It was one of the things that attracted me to him—once I'd finally found it out. You could call it love at hundredth sight.

After Rome we both continued on our separate seasons, sometimes running in the same meet, other times not. I remember one occasion, when I was at training camp in Nice, France, while Tim was competing in Stockholm, Sweden. I was sitting in my hotel room with Chandra, watching the Stockholm meet,

▶ *Tim, mid-race in the 100m final, which I was lucky enough to catch in person.*

when the TV camera focused on Tim warming up before his race. He turned and blew a kiss right into the camera. Chandra, who didn't know about us, was totally confused. "Who the hell's *that* for?" she said. I knew exactly who it was for. So did Trevor, who was in Sweden with Tim, and, as Tim told me later, Trevor blew up at him: "What do you think you're doing? You should be focusing!" Tim ran a 10.08 and won the race.

By late in the 2002 season, both Tim and I were having major conflicts with Trevor. He hated us being together, and the closer we got, the worse Trevor's attitude seemed to get. It wasn't as if we were flaunting our relationship at the track—we were never seen holding hands or acting lovey-dovey, but we weren't hiding anything either. It would have been easy to conceal it if we'd wanted to, since there were about 300 of us training together at this point. (Okay, I'm exaggerating.) I wasn't happy with the overcrowding or with Trevor's autocratic one-prescription-fits-all training methods. And he was really phoning it in. I remember one meet in Brussels, for example. When Tim and I came to the track for practice, Trevor was wearing headphones—which he kept on the entire time. I wrote him a letter after that, since he was still avoiding any discussions with me. I wrote him five or six such letters that season, all saying the same thing: *You need to talk to me. I'm reaching out. I've called you, I've tried to talk on the track . . .* but I never got a single response.

The 2002 season culminated at the World Cup in Madrid, but before that came the Grand Prix Final in Paris. We call that one the "money meet" because you win $60,000 for first place and you also get a number-one ranking, which means bonuses and probably endorsements. For Tim to be ranked number one in the world would have been major; the pressure was intense, especially since reporters had been saying negative things about him—that he couldn't step up in a big meet, that he couldn't beat the top guys.

My 100m final was directly before Tim's, and I won, so I was running the press gauntlet between the track and the seats when Tim was up to race. I really wanted to watch so I begged away from the reporters in time to see him. He can be really nonchalant sometimes, and he was that way before this race. "I'm just gonna run," he shrugged. When he got to his lane—number five, the same one I had—he was so relaxed that he didn't even bother adjusting the blocks to his setting. Then they were off; Tim ran a great race and won. I looked over at the clock to check his time. It read 9.78. In Europe especially, it seems that the clock can malfunction from a strong wind or something like that, so when you see a mind-blowing time you assume the clock is going to correct itself. The last thing you think is "world record." But the clock never changed. I was stunned. "Oh, my gosh," I said to no one in particular. "Tim just broke the 100-meter world record!"

When I looked for him, I saw that he was over the moon at beating everybody. He'd crossed the finish line and gone straight to the reporters, pointing at them and boasting: "See? Told you so!" He hadn't even looked at the clock. Then he realized the crowd was going crazy, and he did sort of a double take, looked at the clock and saw that it read: NEW WR 9.78. He just pulled down his body suit, then Trevor was racing toward him and picked him up. And dropped him. And Tim turned his ankle. It was a bad sprain, but Tim couldn't tell; he was on such a high. He did a victory lap, came right up to me and gave me a big hug—and then we kissed. And the whole world knew. I have a photograph of that moment with Tim and me in an embrace, and Trevor clearly visible behind us, wearing a deep and bitter scowl. If everyone had to find out about Tim and me, it certainly wasn't a bad way to announce it, even if it meant every major newspaper and CNN and NBC and BBC and Canal Plus and so on had roughly the same headline: *World's Fastest Couple!*

◀ *Trevor and I worked well together for six years before we both needed a change. Here we are in Florida during a training session in 1999.*

"I'M JUST G

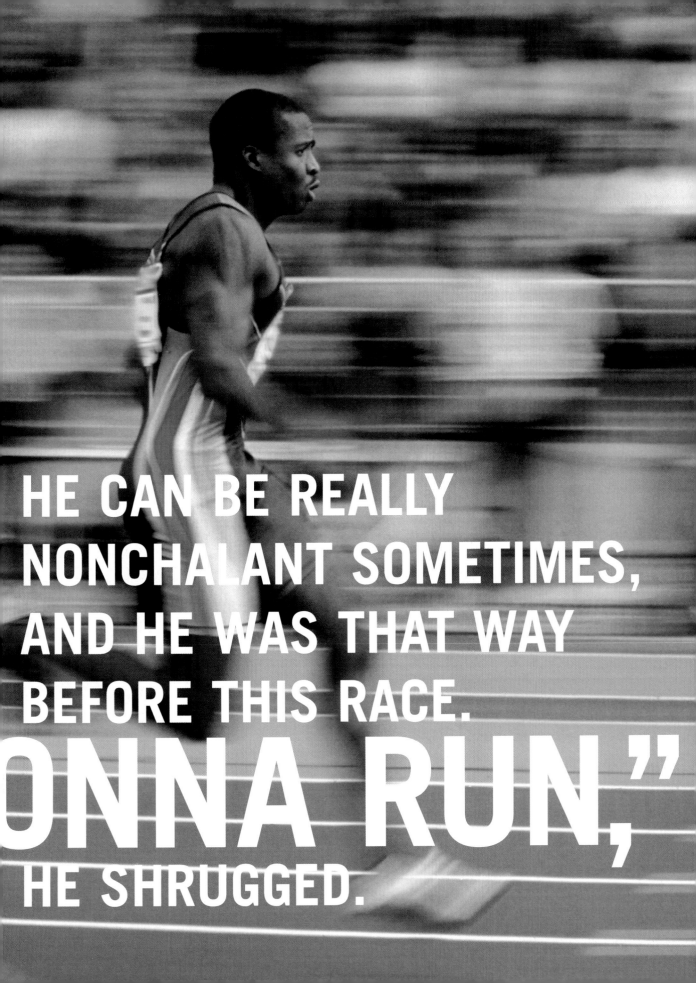

HE CAN BE REALLY
NONCHALANT SOMETIMES,
AND HE WAS THAT WAY
BEFORE THIS RACE.
ONNA RUN,"
HE SHRUGGED.

Tim's season was done after he set the world record—not only because of the ankle, but his body just blew up after the 9.78; you need serious recovery time after a run like that. But I had one more race, the World Cup 100m in Madrid. Normally before a race, Trevor says and does certain things in my warm-up, but I blew him off and warmed up in silence. I didn't want to hear anything from two-faced Trevor anymore. Everything out of his mouth seemed fake. I won, completing my first undefeated season. I'd won the 100m sixteen times, the 200m four times and the 400m once. I was pleased; of course I was. But I knew I hadn't run the best I could possibly run. I'd been distracted, unfocused. Still, I realized that if nobody beat me *this* year when I had so much else going on, then when I got myself back together . . . I was going to give 'em hell.

While I went home to Raleigh, Tim was in New York doing a media tour after his world-record run. One night, speaking on the phone, he told me, "Trevor just called. He said I wasn't allowed back in the group." That was no great shock. By this time, Tim didn't want to be in the group in any case. The question was, What was I going to do? I can only guess that Trevor thought that by getting rid of Tim, things would go back to the way they were between him and me. I think he was in denial about Tim and me. He figured I was on the rebound from C.J. and that Tim was just playing the field. I knew Trevor thought he and I were still doing fine, since he'd given me a letter asking to renegotiate his contract again. This time, I found the number so outrageous that I had to laugh. I mentioned the request to my attorney while I mulled it all over.

Before I'd resolved anything with Trevor, Tim and I decided a vacation was in order, and we went to Maui. There were no hang-ups, no hiding from cameras anymore. We had an amazing time. And the trip sort of made us official in our own eyes. We were together all the time after that and spent Thanksgiving at home in Raleigh with my mom. For Christmas, I went with Tim to be introduced to his family in South Carolina—I'd met his parents when they visited him one weekend, but I got the entire clan this time (minus Tim's two kids, two-year-old Tamaya, who's in Indianapolis, and Jamison, who's five and lives in Virginia). It was a little overwhelming at first because I didn't grow up with the controlled chaos of a big family environment like that. Conversely, it was an adjustment for Tim to be comfortable around my mom, with her reserved ways. But eventually, we both relaxed around each other's families.

Also, by the end of October, negotiations between my attorney and Trevor reached a standstill. It was clear that Trevor and I would have to meet, no matter how uncomfortable that made him. To minimize the intimidation factor—in both directions—we agreed to meet away from each other's houses, and I rented a conference room at a hotel in Raleigh called the Brownstone Hotel. We sat down and tried to start our talks, but the conversation didn't go so well. At some point, Trevor broke down crying.

"Marion, I want to apologize for the past few years," he told me. "I've been going through a rough time—personal problems. I'm sorry. I know I haven't said anything to you about it." I was moved but not distracted. "I'm sorry to hear about that, Trevor," I said. "I feel for you. You know I've had a lot of personal problems of my own. But we're not here to discuss that. We're here to talk business."

"Okay," Trevor said, pulling himself together. "You make a lot of money. I'm aware you make in a single meet what I'm asking for, so I think that's the least I could ask for. After all, I'm the reason for a lot of your success."

"You're the reason for some of my success, Trevor," I said. "But there are a lot of factors involved. You're one of them, but I think what I'm paying you covers that."

"I'm not budging on that figure," he said.

▶ Trevor Graham, who was coaching Tim and me at the time, picked up Tim in celebration after the world-record run. A moment later he dropped Tim, which resulted in a freak ankle twist.

◀ Tim didn't notice that he'd set the world record at first, but the clock told the tale.

▲ Ben Johnson, the Canadian sprinter formerly trained by Charlie Francis, was stripped of his 100m gold medal from the 1988 Seoul Olympics after he tested positive for steroids.

▶ The storm that surrounded Tim and me while Charlie Francis advised us disrupted our lives too much, so we had to part ways.

"Listen, Trevor," I said, annoyed now. "It's because of me you have all these athletes in your group. You're a world-renowned coach. You travel the world. Would all that have happened without me? I'm not prepared to budge either." Then I mentioned being unhappy to hear that he told people I'd trained insufficiently. He denied ever saying that. I decided not to bring up anything Tim had told me, but I laid out more grievances of mine that were concrete. Then I referred him to a proposal that I'd discussed with my attorney. I told him to take it to his attorney, think it over and get back to me. In the end, he rejected my offer and we parted ways by the end of the year. He was no longer my coach.

I'm not quite sure what I would have done had he agreed to the proposal from my attorney, because I was fed up with the situation and unhappy with his coaching. I think in the back of my mind, I knew we wouldn't come to terms. He thought I needed him more than I did, and that I'd have no alternative but to pay him whatever he asked. I'm sure he was angry the way it turned out, because he tried to retaliate by threatening a lawsuit against me, saying I still owed him money from the beginning of the season. Our attorneys sorted out the situation and nothing significant came of it.

When Trevor threw Tim out, I think he was issuing an ultimatum, challenging me to choose between them. And he thought my loyalty to him, Trevor, would win out because of our long history together. I guess Trevor still couldn't believe that Tim and I were having a real relationship—or else he was turning a blind eye to it. He certainly didn't know Tim and I were planning on living together. In early 2003, about a month after we'd moved into Tim's new condo in Raleigh, Trevor came visiting one more time, attempting to reopen discussions with both of us. But I felt we'd said everything there was to say, and we refused to talk to him. For me, the one lingering sadness about that whole sorry tale was the friend I lost in my old training partner, Chandra Sturrup. I sent her an e-mail explaining what had happened and that I hoped it wouldn't affect our relationship. I never heard back. I have to assume her loyalty stayed with Trevor. I miss her.

The upshot of all this was that suddenly Tim and I were both in dire need of a coach for the following season—a crucial season for both of us. We each wanted to solidify and build on the positions we'd reached in 2002. It would be hard to find a coach to take us to the next level. There were only a few who were qualified—maybe three in the whole world—and they were already working with other top athletes. We went back and forth wondering who we'd feel comfortable with out of the handful who might be available. We had a lot of trouble coming up with a name. Eventually we narrowed the field to one: Charlie Francis. A lot of people recognize him as one of the best track and field minds out there—and we wanted to learn from the best. He was particularly known for his highly technical, almost mathematical approach to sprinting, and this is exactly what we felt we needed. We decided that Charlie would not be our coach, but for a while we would have him advise us on and supervise our workouts.

When we made the decision, I didn't really know the specifics of the Charlie Francis story. I was 12 when the Ben Johnson scandal broke, which was a little young to take in the controversy. And frankly, it was the last thing on my mind to wonder whether our new adviser might have ever been in trouble with the IAAF or the Canadian authorities. And even though I learned about Mr. Francis's history, I didn't think it would affect us. In case you missed it too, Charlie Francis was Ben Johnson's coach during the 1988 Seoul Olympics, when Johnson was stripped of his 100m gold medal for failing his drug test. Because he admitted giving steroids to Johnson, Charlie was banned for life from coaching Canadian athletes by Canada's track and field federation in 1989. Ever since, his name has been tainted even though he's spoken out against drugs. It seemed so simple at first—we were going to get advice from the best in the business. Little did we know that the virtual threat of a life ban from some of the biggest international track meets in the world for Tim and me was in the making.

In December 2002, we were still blissfully ignorant of the storm brewing around us even though when we went to Canada and started working with Mr. Francis, one of the first things he said to us was that we should prepare ourselves for some possible media noise, and we should decide what we'd do if we had to stop working with him. We didn't think twice about it, though, because it didn't seem as if his history should have any bearing on our decision. Charlie Francis turned out to be an intense, reserved individual—he reminded me slightly of the genius mathematician Russell Crowe played in *A Beautiful Mind* (without the mental illness!)—and to my delight, he was focused to the point of obsession on the minutest details of sprinting. He had computer programs that digested reams of data to decipher what your angles should be according to your body type at each separate meter of a race. He would film us and analyze our positions, sometimes sitting up all night so that he'd be ready with the correct advice in the morning session. Sometimes he got a little *too* technical and I'd have to stop him to say, "Okay Charlie, you need to slow down here!" We had a very good rapport, but he and Tim really saw eye to eye and spent ages discussing the techie details. We got to know his wife and young son too, since sometimes Charlie would invite us home for dinner—she was a truly excellent cook!

So we trained and it seemed everything was going well—except for the cold, which I hate. In truth, I hated Canada (for the climate only!), and I blamed my uncharacteristic sluggishness there on the freezing temperatures at first. I trained hard, as usual, and did very well. But when I'd return to the hotel, I'd be too exhausted even to go to lunch. The tired feeling didn't abate, and even though I didn't understand why I wasn't able to recover, I wasn't worried. I put it down to the new training system. My body's adjusting to a different regimen, I thought, and to the cold. But when Tim had to go to San Diego for a Nike function and I went with him—to feel the sun and see my home state—I couldn't even hold my head up on the plane ride. I got a little concerned. When we connected through Edmonton, I called my general practitioner back home to have her recommend a doctor in San Diego, just to see what was up. As soon as we deplaned I picked up her message, and while Tim went to the hotel to do his Nike stuff, I went straight to the doctor.

The doctor did tests for viruses, blood-sugar levels, for this and that, but the only test that came up positive was one I hadn't asked for. "I think you're pregnant," he said.

I was incredulous. *Pregnant?* That possibility hadn't crossed my mind for a second. No way was I pregnant! I mean, we'd always been careful. But as the news sank in, I realized it made perfect sense. *This* was the change my body had been experiencing, *this* explained my exhaustion. Just to make sure, the doctor took me to El Dorado hospital in Sandy Hook for an ultrasound, and there was the little peanut-shaped fetus. I was pregnant all right—about two months pregnant. The doctor was great. He could tell I was in mild shock, so he took me back to the hotel and made sure I was okay. I ordered some dinner from room service and waited for Tim to return. An eon later, he strolled in. I held up the ultrasound picture.

"Guess what?" I said.

We sat up and talked for half the night. I cried a lot. I always wanted to be a mom. When I was 21 and 22, I wanted to be a mom someday in the future. Then all of the sudden I was 27 years old. Whoa! Where did the time go? The years between had flashed past in a blur. And now I was pregnant. It was not in the plan, but Tim and I decided: Let's make the most of it. It was meant to happen. Abortion, by the way, was not an option. I don't believe in it. That's my personal choice. I wouldn't dream of forcing my views on anyone else—everybody's situation is different. But for us there was no question. We were going to have a baby.

I HAVE ALWAYS BEEN UNEQUIVOCAL IN MY OPINION: I AM AGAINST PERFORMANCE-ENHANCING DRUGS. I HAVE NEVER TAKEN THEM AND I NEVER WILL TAKE THEM.

It seemed obvious that we shouldn't publicly announce my pregnancy. We could both do without the publicity, and I was intent on continuing to train at a high level—which the doctors said was okay. So we went to spend Christmas with Tim's family—who we told, of course, and they were delighted. Afterward, we went back to Canada, then on to Hawaii to train with help from Charlie Francis. But trouble was just ahead.

To be honest, the fuss made about our new adviser seemed ridiculous to me, especially because my priorities were radically rearranged with a child on the way. Tim and I were portrayed as "playing with fire" because of Charlie's past. Some of the directors of the Golden League meets—the world's top seven elite meets—wanted to blackball us by withholding invitations to compete in 2003. That's why I vowed never to compete in the meet of the ringleader of this group again unless he also paid for the college education of my son and my nieces. (So if you ever see me running in Oslo, you'll know Monty, Iman and Olivia are quite taken care of.) The IAAF spokesman wondered why we'd chosen this man over the "hundreds of excellent sprint coaches in the United States." All the finger-pointing and guilt-by-association implications seemed so petty, so sophomoric. Charlie Francis has renounced the use of performance-enhancing drugs and admitted he was wrong to assist Johnson in taking them. And many major sprinting coaches in the world have consulted, or continue to consult, with him, because he's an authority in the field. Yet nobody wants to admit it. Also, I have always been unequivocal in my opinion: I am against performance-enhancing drugs. I have never taken them and I never will take them. Secure in that knowledge, it didn't occur to me I should fear being associated with this expert coach who had spoken out against drugs and who had been involved with so many of my peers. The hypocrisy of it all was staggering.

News of the controversy we were causing seemed far off at first, but it began to dog us. We were told to be responsible for the image of our sport. I was told I should be careful, since my "golden girl image" (which was hardly *my* invention!) was already tainted by what happened with C.J. in Sydney. Trevor Graham acted put off and aggravated, claiming that we'd left him suddenly, without reason, and he couldn't imagine what we were thinking working with Francis.

Meanwhile, Tim and I were training incessantly. My exhaustion disappeared after the first trimester, and I stepped up the pace. But when we returned from Hawaii, we were getting fed up with all the fuss about Charlie, so we thanked him profusely for his work and parted ways. People think we succumbed to pressure from the track and field community and our sponsors, but that's not the case at all. We were simply fed up of being stalked by cameras 24/7—especially Tim, who was training harder than I was by this time. People would literally wait behind the bushes hoping for a glimpse of one of us with Charlie. The people at Nike never pressured either of us in any way. They didn't love the negative press, but they knew we'd make the correct decision. Even the IAAF was fine once they'd talked to us directly rather than relying on hearsay. Only USATF failed to rescind their vote of no confidence, once again proving how good they are at being nice to you when they need you, then turning their back at the first whiff of controversy. The funny thing was, if those critics had known I was four months pregnant, they'd have realized there was no way I was going anywhere near any kind of drug. And keeping me out of the 2003 Golden League was no threat. Little did they know that Marion Jones was not going to have a 2003 season at all.

◀ *My pregnancy changed everything and gave me a lot of perspective about the media storm that surrounded Tim and me leading up to the 2003 season.*

# 10.

# MONTY

Two thousand three was not exactly the ideal time to take a temporary retirement. I was at a crucial stage in my career. It was the year before the Athens Olympics. I'd just left my coach after six years. I hadn't lost in 2002, but I honestly didn't consider it a good year on the track. However, by new year's I'd done a great deal of thinking and I was a hundred percent sure Tim and I were doing the right thing having a baby. On the track, sure, I wouldn't be roaring back into competition like a lion, like I'd hoped, but my time would come round again. In fact, they say pregnancy and childbirth can actually improve your athletic performance. I was going to be finding out if that was true.

We'd told Tim's family about the baby at Christmas, but I had to tell all the people close to me. I was worried most about telling my mom because I didn't know how she'd react. She'd never been the "When-are-you-going-to-give-me-some-grandbabies?" type. Except once, in 2001, when she asked it as a kind of a joke and I teased her back, "You'd better get used to Izzy"---that's my little dog---"because she's going to be your only grandchild from me." But even if she'd secretly wanted grandchildren all along, I worried that now she would think I was jeopardizing my career, or maybe she'd disapprove of an out-of-wedlock child. Either way, I knew she'd be even more surprised than I was back in November.

In the end, I was six months pregnant when I finally told her. It turned out that my brother and his wife had a baby on March 3, 2003, so mom was staying with them in California, helping out. I didn't want to tell her over the phone, so I waited until she came home to Raleigh in early April. When I picked her up from the airport, she didn't know a thing. At the time, I was showing but you couldn't tell under the baggy clothes I always wear. When we got to her place, she wanted to go out and eat as we normally would, but I stalled. "No, mom," I said. "Let's just stay in this afternoon. I've got to talk to you about something." Then I told her I wasn't going to compete this year. "That's probably a good idea," she said. "You could use a break after your last two seasons." Oh goodness. She wasn't making this easy. In the end, I just blurted out, "Mom, I'm gonna have a baby." At first, she didn't say anything; she just looked at me. I held my breath. When she spoke, she asked me simply, "Marion, is this what you want? Are you happy?" I grinned. "Yes mom," I said.

And she gave me a huge hug.

After that, she was so excited. All of the sudden, *boom!* she was having two grandkids in one year. She couldn't have been happier. It was a big weight off my shoulders, too. Now all I had to do was tell the rest of the world.

Tim and I were enjoying the peace of keeping my pregnancy quiet, and we decided to keep that going as long as possible. I say "enjoying," but while we were still in Canada, in December and January, I was miserable. I'd break down crying now and again because not only did I hate the place and the cold, but I hate cities too and I hate not being independent, and we had to rely on cabs, or on Charlie Francis driving us around. Maybe it was also raging hormones. When we decamped for training camp at Honolulu University in Hawaii---with Charlie again---I was entering my second trimester, and things looked up. I had a surge of energy, and we were training at a really high level. Still nobody but Tim and I (and his family) knew. Not even Charlie.

When we came home after Hawaii, we were really scrambling. Since Tim and I had both left Trevor, we didn't have a place to train and we didn't have a full-time coach---since, contrary to what was being suggested in the press, Charlie was still just advising us on workouts. Also, this is when we began to get eaten alive by the press, by USA Track & Field and the IAAF. Mostly I managed to tune out the grumbling and just keep on training. We'd found the perfect facility—a private academy whose athletic director was gung-ho about Tim and me using the track—where we still train today. I was feeling great.

In mid-April, I publicly announced my pregnancy and that I'd miss the 2003 season. Tim bore the brunt of the press attention—not only about Charlie, but about me and Tim Jr.—and it started to take a toll on him. I stayed at home, reading every pregnancy book I could get my hands on, studying how a baby looks at week 22, 25, 28—and sneaking peaks at weeks 32 and 35 because I was so excited. I'd stopped running on the track back in March because it had gotten uncomfortable, but I could still use the treadmill; after all, they can only go so fast. My doctor encouraged me. As long as you're fit before you were pregnant, she said, you can do anything. Just stop at the first sign of discomfort. So that's what I did. I ran on the treadmill and lifted weights, and I didn't have to stop very often. I could run the same workouts Charlie had taught me, and with the lifting, I just increased the reps and decreased the weight.

There was a YMCA right next to our condo in North Raleigh, so that's where I'd go every day. I got to be good friends with the morning regulars, mostly older men and women. They were kind of proud to have this Olympic medal winner training there, and I never got bothered, apart from the ladies checking up on me, saying things like: "You're not doing too much, right?" One day, I remember one of the ladies had her granddaughter with her; she was about my age and also pregnant, though not as much as I, and she was jogging gently on the next treadmill. There I was, in my zone, running along, watching the TV, and I heard the lady say to her granddaughter: "Okay, you need to stop that. You know you're not supposed to run when you're pregnant," and the girl nodded at me and they both looked over and I had the thing cranked up to about *eleven*, and I just said, "Hi!" and smiled. And we all cracked up. The girl continued jogging.

Tim was competing overseas a great deal during all those months, so it was really hard for me. Even though my mom was nearby, and Tim's younger brother, Gamar—he runs track and plays football at school—was living with us, and coming with me to the gym, it was a really lonely time. It was difficult for Tim too, because all the press attention was focused on him, and after setting the world record in 2001, he wasn't running well. Tim's not comfortable in front of the media and they wouldn't leave him alone about Charlie Francis, my pregnancy, us not being married, and the split with Trevor—which they were calling Tim's decision, unsurprisingly given what Trevor had let them believe. And there I was, stuck at home, pregnant, and more pregnant, and more pregnant and more pregnant, and Tim would be back for only a few days before he'd be off again. One time, I had a surreal experience. Being a women's basketball fan, I was watching WNBA draft coverage on SportsCenter when they announced a Marion Jones drafted to the Phoenix Mercury. "Cute," I thought. "There's a player with my name." But when they said she was from North Carolina, and then my manager called to tell me I'd been drafted, I realized what had just happened. That's hilarious, I thought. I'm not even running this year, and I haven't played basketball since 1997, but still, it's kind of cool.

Most of my days were far less entertaining than that. The only good part of all this time on my hands was that I was *very* well prepared. I had my bag packed and ready by the door. I'd practiced my breathing—Tim and I had taken classes months before—and I had my labor plan all written out. I wanted only the necessary people in the room, and I didn't want an epidural, unless it got too bad and then I'd decide. I wanted to walk around, and have as few needles in me as possible, and be asked before they did any episiotomy. I also wanted Tim to cut the cord, and I wanted the baby handed to me immediately. Yes, I admit it—in short, I wanted to be in control.

▲ My mother (aka "Big Marion") and my uncle,
Godwin Hulse, accompanied me to the 2000
IAAF gala in Monaco.

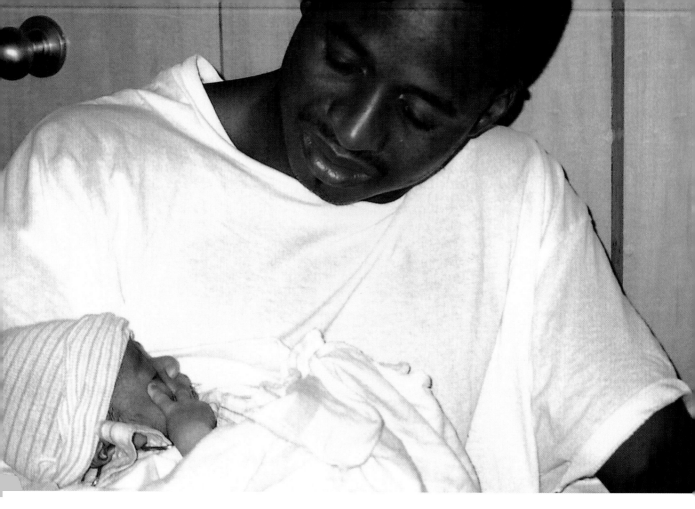

▲ *Tim was at a meet in Scotland when Monty was born early. He raced back as soon as he could and came straight from the airport to the hospital to see his new son.*

# WHEN WE GOT THERE, ABOUT 6 P.M., I WAS SURPRISED TO FIND "OPERATION MARION" FULLY UNDER WAY.

The hospital also had its issues. Since the baby was such a huge deal for the European media, we'd had to sit down with the chiefs of hospital security and PR, the head nurse, my manager, and plan it like a military operation: how to sneak me in when I went into labor; how to monitor people and guard my room 24 hours a day; how to get me out of hospital the back way. It was all mapped out.

With the due date—July 20—rapidly approaching, Tim was still bouncing back and forth from Europe where most meets on the circuit take place. On June 24, he was due to leave for a track meet in Scotland. He was reluctant to go, but we saw the doctor together just before he left. "You know, nothing is guaranteed, and you never know," she said. "But Marion is not having Braxton-Hicks contractions, and she's not even close to dilated, so if you want to travel, go ahead." So off Tim went.

Then at 10 a.m. on Friday, June 27, Gamar came to get me for the gym, which was unusual because it was usually *me* who knocked on *his* door and pestered him to go. I just wasn't feeling up to it, so I stayed home. Then next morning, Saturday, I was going to the bathroom (as you do constantly in the third trimester), when I felt a little water run down my leg. *Oops*, I thought, *didn't make it in time*. And when Gamar came to fetch me for the gym, I was so tired again I told him I might have a little touch of the flu. I mean, I knew about the water breaking, but I didn't know what to expect: Is it a gush of fluids? Is it just drips? I knew I was close, but I had no contractions, no dilation, three full weeks to go and Tim wasn't there. This was not the way I'd planned it!

Gamar went off to the gym, and I sat on the sofa watching television and doing the bills. But every hour I was feeling . . . *something*. Not pain, not even pressure, but just a little twinge, Monty was rolling perhaps. No big deal. But at 4 p.m., it was getting stronger, so I called the doctor and said: "It's probably nothing, but there was a little leaking this morning."

"Okay," she said, "you need to come to the hospital."

"Are you sure, Dr. Ford? You know, it's a long trip." The hospital was Duke, which was a good half hour's drive away.

"Just humor me," she said. "Come on over."

So I quietly called my contact at the hospital for a heads-up, just to say I was coming in so we could talk more about the plan. I found Tim's brother and said, quite breezily, "Hey, Gamar, I'm not feeling too good. Can you take me to my doctor?"

We got in the truck . . . and the tank was empty. At this point I felt the pressure increasing but still we drove, chatting casually. We stopped for gas, and just as we were pulling out of the station, my phone rang. It was Tim. I hadn't been able to reach his cell phone in Scotland, so he had no idea.

"Hey, how you doing?" he said.

So I said, all calmly, "Okay, Tim, don't panic, alright? But I'm on my way to the hospital." There was no pause.

"*What?* Oh my gosh, I'm gonna find a flight *right now*."

But I said, "Look, you've made a commitment to those meet promoters. The race is in the morning. Just run it and then come home." By this time, the pressure of the contractions was really mounting and Gamar was so busy chatting to me, he didn't notice that he was slowing down, so I gently suggested that, hey, he might need to pick it up just a little.

When we got there, about 6 p.m., I was surprised to find "Operation Marion" fully under way. I wasn't there to give birth, but security had still taken care of everything: my two designated nurses, a secluded room at the end of the hall. . . . In fact, I must say, from start to finish, this hospital's security, the nurses and the doctors handled every part of my demanding birth schedule *so* well that I can never thank them enough. And this was my first glimpse of their spectacular professionalism in action. Already, all the arrangements we'd discussed were in place. This is when I realized I might be further along than I thought.

When they measured and discovered I was six centimeters dilated, I really got it. "Okay, Gamar," I said, "I'm going to have this baby tonight. You need to call your parents, get in contact with Tim. . . ."

"WHAT? Okay, man, where do you want me first?" Gamar was all of 20 years old at the time, and Tim had entrusted him with a lot of responsibility. It was so cute how extremely helpful he was, with me squirming on the seat clutching on to a pillow for dear life while the contractions got stronger. But there was one call Gamar couldn't make for me. I dialed the familiar number. "Hi, Mom," I said. "How you doing?"

"Fine," she said.

"Well," I continued, calmly, "don't panic or anything. But I think you should come to the hospital. They say I'm going to have this baby tonight."

"*What?*"

"So, when you get a chance, make your way on over here. . . ."

I can't help smiling, thinking back. Am I calm under pressure, or what?

By then, Gamar had managed to reach Tim and he got through on my cell phone. I told him we were going to have the baby tonight, and he started frantically trying to get a flight. In the end, he couldn't get one until Monday, so of course he didn't sleep at all that night and he ran horribly in his meet. At least when he finally did get to Raleigh, they were ready for him with a police escort to the hospital. Another unexpected thing was my beloved Dr. Ford—who I had relied on exclusively the entire pregnancy, and who I was so sure would deliver Monty personally that I hadn't even bothered to meet any of her partners—was far away at her daughter's camp that weekend and had to find a friend of hers who was on call to deliver my baby.

By the time I was eight centimeters dilated, my mom made it to my side. At first, I wasn't sure how comfortable I'd feel with my mom in the room, but it turned out she was absolutely incredible—so supportive and emotionally strong. I was so grateful she was there. At this point, my contractions were coming one after another without any break at all. Until then I'd been okay with the pain, but it became too much. I probably screamed it at this point: "Give me an epidural!"

I'd had a real fear of epidurals, especially of the needle part, because they make it look so graphic in the classes. And I was also really nervous about it affecting my spine because you do hear horror stories about legs being paralyzed, even temporarily, and so on. But the guy came along, I felt a little prick, hardly

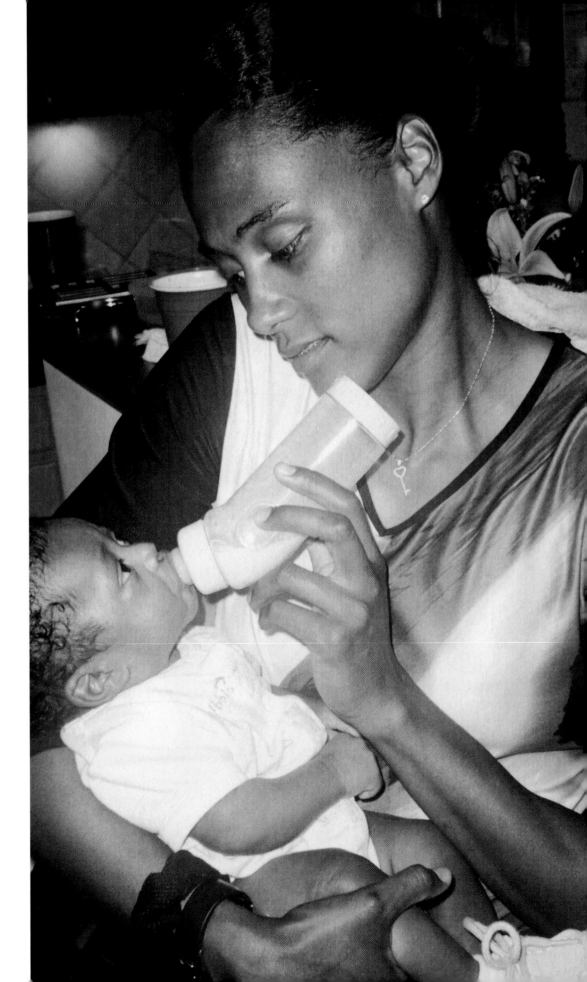

anything at all, and after that there wasn't pain any more, it was just pressure, and I was still able to feel my legs. I wanted to hug him.

At about 9:15 p.m., they measured me again, and I was ten centimeters—fully dilated. "Okay," said the nurse, "You're gonna have a baby."

"What? Right now?" I could hardly believe it.

"Right now. Any time you want to push, you can push."

"I can push *now*?"

"Right now!" And so I started to push. I only remember about four or five hard pushes. Then Monty was there. But all was not well. What the doctor didn't tell me right away was that the longest umbilical cord she had ever seen was wrapped two and a half times around my baby's neck. His heart rate had dropped so low they were on the brink of performing an emergency caesarian. The intensive care team was in the room in any case, since he was so early, so when the doctor cut the cord, they whisked Monty away. I'd been kind of dreading the roomful of people and me there on the table with my legs all spread, but at that point, I couldn't care less. Talk about the zone. There could have been fifty people in the room. The only hard part was that I didn't get to hold my baby the moment he was born.

Timothy Lois Montgomery was born at 9:58 p.m., June 28, 2003. At 9:59 p.m. my cell phone rang and mom answered. I heard her say to someone, "He's born! He's born!" It was Tim. He just happened to pick that moment to call again. Monty was still in the corner, being helped with his breathing, and I kept asking the doctor, "Is everything okay?" because of course the baby has to cry before you know it's all fine. Then it happened, Monty cried. And Tim was right there; he heard it too. And I was crying—tears of joy. I could finally hold my baby. And he was just so, so perfect and it truly struck me for the first time: Oh, my gosh! I'm a mother!

"You've got a boy," I said to Tim. (We'd learned that early on and I was happy about it. I would have been happy with a girl too, but as I've said over and over, I'm such a tomboy at heart; I'm not into dresses; I don't know how to braid hair. . . .) Some newborns have squishy faces; they could be either gender, but Monty's features were totally masculine. I was laughing and crying. I told Tim on the phone: "He's *such* a boy!"

The PR machine sprang into action then and made a statement to the press, and the next morning I was sitting in my room with Monty in my arms, watching the news on TV. And there we were: *Tim Montgomery, world record holder, and Marion Jones, Olympic gold medalist, had a baby blah blah blah. . . .* and they were making the predictable jokes about how fast he was already, three weeks early. Then the silly anchor lady said to the co-anchor, *Now, that baby sure is going to have pressure on him to succeed. . . .*

And I was upset because Monty was sitting there, wide awake. So I looked him in the eyes and I said, "Hey little buddy, don't listen to her. You don't have any pressure on you at all. Whatever you want to do in life, you can do it."

And I flipped off the TV.

◀ *While the arrival of Monty wasn't exactly planned, becoming a parent for the first time has been the most amazing experience of my life so far.*

11.

ERHOOD

I WAS TERRIFIED BECAUSE NOBODY KNEW WHAT WAS CAUSING MONTY'S PROBLEMS.

Monty was two days old when we brought him home from the hospital. He was four days old when we brought him back. It was only to see the pediatrician for his mandatory checkup. All was fine until later that evening, when Dr. Salter, the pediatrician, called. "You have to take Monty to hospital right now," he said. "The baby has jaundice. His bilirubin count is extraordinarily high."

Newborn jaundice, I found out later, is extremely common. In most cases the problem goes away without the need for medical attention. In Monty's case, it didn't—and I became an instant expert. I learned that Monty's bilirubin (a waste product of the breakdown of red blood cells) was processed by my liver through the placenta until his birth. Afterward, his tiny liver wasn't able to cope fast enough. The bilirubin count always climbs in the first days of life, peaking around day four—and Monty's had apparently soared to 28. A count higher than 20 can lead to brain damage. We were about to pass the worst few nights of our lives.

We rushed our son to Duke's ER, where a nurse proceeded to take a blood test—only he was so tiny (5 pounds, 11 ounces) that she couldn't find a vein. Tim, who's phobic about needles, turned away as the nurse poked around him from wrist to heel trying to find a spot. When nothing worked and she was about to stab the vein in his forehead, I broke down in tears. I couldn't bear it. Thank goodness the doctor appeared then and managed to get a needle in his ankle. He took some

blood and started Monty on phototherapy, which involved placing him under a sunlamp on a special blanket. The UV light from the lamp is supposed to help break down the bilirubin. But it didn't work for Monty. Early in the morning, the doctor decided to perform a blood transfusion—to take out all of our tiny baby's blood and replace it with a stranger's blood. We were horrified. It seemed so extreme.

I thought it couldn't get much worse until we got to the ICU. There were babies there with terminal illnesses, kids who were on their last breath. In the waiting room I heard a doctor tell some fellow parents that they had to talk to their son, because he was dying. *Thank God,* I thought. *We're the lucky ones.* At least, I hoped we were.

I was terrified because nobody knew what was causing Monty's problems. I was only allowed into the ICU to see him every few hours, and he was lying there listlessly every time I went in. After the first night, I sent Tim home to train and to see his folks, who had come up from South Carolina to meet their new grandson. For about 24 hours, I paced back and forth, stared at the TV, dozed, turned the pages of my book without taking in a word. I was a wreck.

Finally, the transfusion was completed and Monty was moved to another part of the ICU, where I was allowed to stay. He was really weak, but gradually he was able to take milk, and the fluids revived him. The doctors kept checking him and telling us, "Okay, this evening, he'll probably be released." Then they'd keep him another night. Though I was desperate to get him out of there, I didn't want to be pushy or, worse, put my baby in any danger. In the end, we stayed five nights.

Finally, we learned what had probably been behind Monty's jaundice, and why it had taken so long to cure. It turned out there'd been a mix-up. When they took Monty's blood at birth, I was told he had my blood type, but that had been a mistake. He had Tim's blood type, and he also had a G6PD deficiency (a problem with enzymes that arises from a disorder that one in 10 of African-American men have—without even knowing it in most cases). All it boils down to is that Monty has to avoid a short list of medications and foods. He will never eat fava beans his whole life long. There are worse things.

We continued to visit the pediatrician every day for weeks, getting blood tests and ear tests (very high bilirubin can affect the child's hearing), and we sat Monty by the window to catch the sunlight. He's been fine ever since. And people wondered why Tim Montgomery had a poor season in 2003. He must be out of shape, they said. They had no idea.

After the scare, we adjusted easily to life with Monty. I had decided to give myself a month after he was born to establish a rhythm with him, and allow my body time to recover before getting back into training. And it turned out that Monty was agreeable to that plan, too. We were blessed with an easy baby. He'd wake up a few times at night, as all newborns do, but from the first, he was never a screaming, crying baby. Whenever he wanted something he'd do a little "eh eh" noise—we called it his little bird cry—or he'd whine gently. There was only one evening early on when he screamed for about 20 minutes. We were so unaccustomed to it that Tim and I didn't know what the heck to do. While I was home with him, I was also visiting my doctor regularly, awaiting her go-ahead. At the end of July, she pronounced me ready to begin training again. Just start slowly, she warned.

When Tim and I stopped consulting with Charlie Francis back in February, Tim started training with Llewellyn Starks, who worked with Charlie Wells at Vector Sports. Llewellyn was a great long jumper until a compound leg fracture ended his career, and he also knew sprinting, so he was a great help to Tim. But he was more someone to be out there with a watch and a knowledgeable eye; he wasn't a coach. When Tim asked him to help us find one, Llewellyn suggested we try his former coach, Dan Pfaff, who had been at the University of Texas for a number of years. I knew the name. Dan had an impressive reputation from training, among others, Kareem Streete-Thompson, Obadele Thompson from Barbados, Sevatheda Fynes from the Bahamas, and the Canadian 100m sprinters Donovan Bailey and Bruny Surin. We called him.

Dan said it would be hard to get out of his contract at the University of Texas, but he was happy to hear our proposal. Around late April, we flew him to Raleigh and told him he was just what we needed— someone with a sprinting background who was also technically sound in jumping. We asked if he would be able to move if we made a sweet enough offer. He felt bad about the prospect of leaving some of his athletes and also had concerns about job security and benefits and about uprooting his family, but, in time, we worked it all out. Dan moved to Raleigh in July.

▲ Tim and I usually practice in the mornings then come straight home to be with Monty after our workouts are done.

▶ The grandmothers are invaluable to Tim and me, always watching over Monty when we practice and travel. Here, Monty and my mom share a moment.

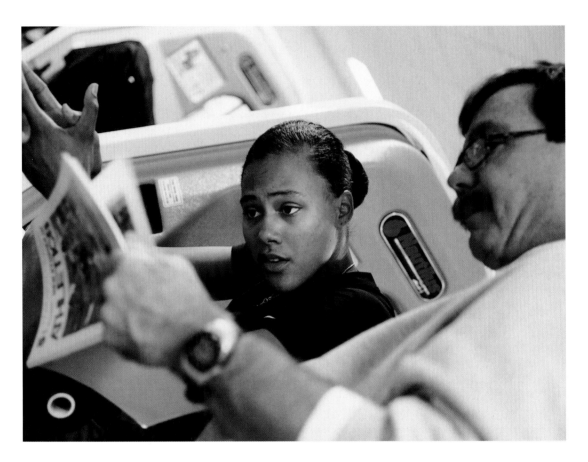

▲ *Monty wasn't the only new person to arrive in my life in 2003. Tim and I hired a new coach, Dan Pfaff, who had previously been coaching at the University of Texas.*

My return to the track and our new coach's arrival coincided nicely. In many ways it was a terrible risk to start with a new coach in an Olympic year, as adjusting to a new system and unfamiliar techniques could take some time. But it was obvious right away that Dan was going to work out just fine. My first day back I was as excited as a child waking up on Christmas morning. I was brimming over, ready to do six 300s. Practically the first thing Dan told me as my coach was, "Slow down! My wife would kill me if she knew I had you working out already." Our first days consisted mostly of learning Dan's warm-ups and drills, which were different from Trevor's, plus some stretching and some light jogging. Also unlike Trevor, Dan explained exactly how and why we should be doing every little thing, and what the benefits of each were. I felt just fine. I had, after all, been training until two days before Monty's birth.

In the second week, Dan started to incorporate bounding, which is exactly how it sounds—long, high, slow strides over grass. It was when I felt my first postchildbirth twinges. My uterus, of course, had not yet made it back to its starting position, so every time I landed from a bound, I'd feel a little "woops!" It was not great for my bladder. But aside from that, my body sprang back remarkably fast. My stomach had flattened more or less in a day—at least when I was lying down. (The hospital nurses let me know how they hated me for that!) Three weeks after Monty was born, I'd lost 25 pounds and was back to my prepregnancy weight of 157 pounds. Training removed another couple of pounds. To reach my ideal running weight, 150-odd pounds, I modified what I ate.

My diet seems to be a big curiosity to people, but the awful truth is that I really don't follow any special regime. I'm pretty cavalier about food and always have been. A typical day's menu is as follows: Breakfast is a bowl of grits with butter and sugar, plus maybe a slice of toast and a scrambled egg. That's my fuel for training—about three hours. Then I have the main meal of the day: grilled pork chops or steamed fish or roast chicken. Sometimes Tim will get a craving so we'll stop off at the store for, say, smoked turkey legs and macaroni and cheese, which he'll cook when we get home. After having dinner for lunch, I'll just pick at leftovers later on, or sometimes we'll go out for some light supper. And at some point I'll have dessert. Always dessert.

Always . . . for now. That summer, as I began training with Dan, and as I planned the bigger picture for 2004 with Nike and Charlie Wells, and also supervised construction of my house and, above all, got to know Monty, I had no time to worry about what I ate. I had too much going on. In the new year, my training would step up to include more hard-core, longer-distance running (though never longer than 400 meters, and hardly ever more than 300 meters in practice—the longest distance I have ever run in my life is probably a quarter mile). That's when I would get down to fighting weight. To achieve that, I'd restrict myself to dessert just two times a week. I'd cut out the toast and eggs in the morning. I'd have a sandwich—with turkey, no mayonnaise—after training and delay the main meal till five or six, so my stomach would be empty by bedtime. And I'd drink a lot of water to make me feel full. Simple, sensible, effective.

By the end of August I was really back in a good training rhythm. And "rhythm" is the right word. Dan got rid of my rigid, three-phase pounding, and led me into a more fluid, *rhythmic* style. He said, at 5'11" with my "long levers" (legs, that is), I wasn't a power sprinter and shouldn't be slamming my feet down on the track. I was primed for change thanks to Charlie Francis, who had already shown me how my old style wasn't right for my body type. For a start—and *at* the start—he'd had me widen the setting on my blocks so that my crouch was less cramped. Now Dan continued the work of opening out and loosening up a style that had seemed to work for me, but that turned out to have done me no favors.

Dan totally revamped my arch position—the second, "set" part of the start—so that my back leg was almost fully extended and my hips were higher. I no longer had to lavish energy on uncoiling at the gun, but could exploit my length right away. My old explosive technique, he said, was for shorter sprinters. And Dan wanted me to expend effort more evenly throughout a race. He talked about feeling my rhythm and letting my body do what came naturally. I'd been forcing myself into the head-down, slamming the feet, drive-transition-acceleration pattern for so long, it wasn't as easy as it sounds just to allow my body to do its thing. But it felt good.

I know Dan found me a quick study, and that had its drawbacks when it came to the long jump. The last thing I wanted was to pick up fragments here and there and end up as Frankenjumper with cobbled-together technique. So I told Dan, "Please tell me real basic stuff. Don't assume I know things. Start right from the beginning." So we did. And at first it was really frustrating. It was like being back at school when I'd study and study and I'd know the material, yet it wouldn't necessarily come out right when I needed it. Knowing what I was supposed to do was one thing, but getting my body to do it was quite another matter, especially in the air, when I was dealing with gravity as well as velocity. There were many, many sessions when I jumped horribly. But I kept studying the tape we'd film, and I kept getting better.

Dan taught me about the "penultimate." That's the step before takeoff, and it's the key to the whole thing. You'd think the most important part of the long jump is the landing or the takeoff or technique in the air—and sure, that all matters—but the penultimate allows you to get your body in position to kick your leg up and assume the correct form. That is the make-or-break moment. Before Dan, I relied solely on my speed down the runway to propel me forward, like a race with the last part airborne. Dan taught me to control that speed. I had to contain the velocity I'd generated in the run-up during a four-step drive into the jump. Coming out of those four steps, I learned to find the board with my eyes and steer my body into the exact center, then, on the penultimate, to lower my center of gravity very slightly by bending my knees and then launch from my left foot, heel first, heel-to-toe, and kick my right leg straight out. It was precise, and it was terribly challenging. Dan said I had a tendency to "toe it" off the board because I brought so much speed down the runway, and that this propelled me forward too fast and made me fling myself in the pit. Which is, of course, what I always used to do. That's how I managed to hyperextend my knee back in 1999 at the Pontiac Grand Prix. I retained a fear in the back of my mind that I'd do that again, that if I stretched out my legs, my knees wouldn't bend on landing, though now that I was sliding instead of slamming into the pit I knew perfectly well that that was no longer a danger.

One thing Dan did that I instantly loved was to give me cues. I could internalize one of these, or repeat it silently like a mantra and, magically, my body would respond. For instance, in the long jump, I persistently dropped my legs when I was over the pit. I thought they were extended straight out, horizontal to the ground, but on tape it was obvious I had a mental blockage there. My legs were droopy. Dan said the problem came from the way I tended to thrust my torso forward, and that I needed to keep my *upper* body straight. "Keep your hands in front," he said. And that worked to correct my form. It was a continual challenge not to revert to my old ways, but finally I had the information I'd craved so desperately. I understood the long jump. My last one in competition had been a foul in the Olympics; now I was looking forward to replacing that painful memory with something that would make me proud.

# DAN EXPLAINED EXACTLY HOW AND WHY WE SHOULD BE DOING EVERY LITTLE THING, AND WHAT THE BENEFITS OF EACH WERE.

▲ Dan Pfaff has a different approach to training than I was used to. He is very flexible and tries to tailor workouts and technique to our individual needs and tendencies.

IT WAS A CONTINUAL
CHALLENGE NOT TO
REVERT TO MY OLD WAYS,
BUT FINALLY I HAD THE
INFORMATION I'D CRAVED
SO DESPERATELY.

We toyed with the idea of my running in a meet that summer of 2003, but it didn't happen. Looking back, I'm very glad, because I wasn't as ready as I thought, but at the time my itch to compete was so intense that it almost overwhelmed my reason. The itch peaked in August, watching Tim run in the World Championships in Paris. Tim ran his fastest time of the year, but ended up placing fifth in the final. Given everything that was going on, we were pleased with that, and we went home happy. Unfortunately Tim came in for a lot of criticism for "deserting" the U.S. 4x100m relay team because he was disappointed with his personal performance. It was unfair because he'd talked to the relay coaches months before and excused himself, explaining how he wasn't running well this season and would be likely to let the team down. They had understood perfectly. Yet here were those same coaches making negative comments about Tim to the press. I can't say I was exactly shocked, but I was—once again—disappointed.

Tim's "crime" was soon overshadowed, though, by another breaking news story. Kelli White, who had just become the first American woman to win both the 100m and 200m at the worlds, had tested positive for a substance called Modafinil. This was a stimulant that wasn't on the banned list at the time (though it was covered by the catchall "and related substances" phrase) and that Kelli White claimed she was taking to combat narcolepsy. Nobody was convinced by that argument. It wasn't long before a few other athletes (Chryste Gaines among them) turned out to have also tested positive for Modafinil. It was suggested that the Modafinil might have been taken as a masking agent for another, more sinister performance-enhancing drug that had first hit the headlines in June, when an anonymous source—a track coach—sent a sample to the U.S. Anti-Doping Agency, USADA, claiming athletes had been taking it because it was undetectable. That so-called "designer steroid" was tetrahydrogestrinone, or THG, and it sparked a storm that continues today. The storm intensified in late summer 2003, when the anonymous coach named the alleged source of THG, and that lab was raided by the narcotics task force and the IRS. The lab was, of course, BALCO, run by my ex-husband C.J.'s pal Victor Conte. I hadn't seen Conte—or heard of him for that matter—since Sydney. But I would soon find that even that tenuous link was enough to give me a part to play in clearing up the whole mess—as much as that is ever possible in the foul world of performance-enhancing drugs.

My dream home was finally ready in November 2003. As I mentioned earlier, it was the first investment in something personal I'd ever made—and it was a significant one. Ever since I was about 10 years old I've been fascinated by houses, devouring shelter magazines and even touring model homes. All along I stored away details I liked with the idea: *That's what I'll have in my own home one day.* Needless to say, when it came time to design and build, I had strong opinions about everything from color schemes to layout. For instance, I didn't want 15 bedrooms (I don't have that many friends!), but I did want a fitness room and a playroom with a pool table. I also wanted a room to store all my medals and trophies and newspaper articles that was far enough out of the way that I wouldn't have to see it every day. And for years I'd dreamed of having a high-ceilinged, sun-drenched room painted floor to ceiling with murals of the Belizean jungle. But most decadent of all, I wanted a swimming pool. Since I was five years old, it was a dream of mine.

Moving into a new home is a rite of passage that brings up memories and lends perspective. It was humbling to reflect on what had happened to me during the five years since I first started designing my house. I'd become the first woman in history to win five track and field medals in a single Olympics. I'd been divorced. I'd become a mother. And I was in a new relationship that made me very happy. Since the moment we were caught on camera when he broke the 100m world record in Paris, both Tim and I had been barraged with questions from the media about our relationship. Or rather, just the one question: Are you going to get married? (Some reporters bypassed the question altogether and simply wrote about "Marion Jones and her husband, Tim Montgomery.") For the record, we're certainly not going to be pressured into anything—especially not by the media—but we both feel we'll probably want to make it official at some point. On the other hand, everyone knows married couples who are miserable and have children who suffer because of it. A wedding is never a solution to a faltering relationship. Tim and I have the best parts of a marriage already—we love each other, we're happy, our son is happy and our families are happy for us. I'm open-minded about the prospect of marriage—one bad experience didn't put me off the whole institution—but I believe that if two people are responsible and are in a committed relationship, then a certificate and a ring don't make much of a difference.

The Montgomerys and the Joneses are already family anyway. Our new home may not have 15 bedrooms, but it does have one for Tim's mother, Marjorie, and soon after we moved in, she put her own home life on hold and took up temporary residence. In fact, we were very grateful that both of Monty's grandmas were extremely hands-on with Monty while we prepared for the Olympics. My mom was also there from the start, watching Monty in the mornings while we trained and being ready to take over for an evening at a moment's notice. And since we planned to leave Monty at home for most of his first year, the grandmas were full-time caregivers when we started traveling to meets. The chaos of meets and of long-distance travel would be too disruptive for him, especially once we'd managed to get him on a schedule.

One trip Monty did make in his first year was to the Cayman Islands. For the past few years (not 2003, of course) I'd been traveling to Hawaii as a winter training base, but we were made an irresistible offer late in 2003. One of our new training partners who arrived with Dan Pfaff was the 100m sprinter and long jumper Kareem Streete Thompson from the Caymans. Through Kareem, representatives from Grand Cayman offered to put up the whole group of us free of charge for a month. We got hotel rooms for Dan and the athletes, and a condo for Margie, Tim, Monty and me, plus a wonderful track for our workouts. In return, we did a press conference and opened some workouts to the public—which were hugely popular occasions with an almost carnival atmosphere because the Cayman Islanders regard Kareem with the same sort of pride that Belizeans have for me. Overall it was a wonderful experience, one we're definitely thinking of repeating in future off-seasons.

Just before leaving for the Caymans, I had an important task to deal with—I was called to testify before a federal grand jury. Their interest in me dated back to C.J. and Trevor's dealings with Victor Conte of BALCO, who was one of four people indicted in the first stanza of a now-epic saga of doping in the top levels of professional sport. To be frank, I never paid much attention to the nuances of our legal system and wasn't entirely sure what a grand jury did until I met one. But everyone, including my attorney, said not to worry. All I had to do was speak the truth and tell them all I knew. So I flew to San Francisco and awaited my turn. Even though I'd done nothing wrong, the experience was intimidating, sitting alone in front of this large roomful of jurors, answering the U.S. attorney's questions. But I got through. In the end, I was only in there for 40 minutes.

I'm legally bound not to discuss any details of what I learned in that San Francisco court room, which is a little frustrating because some of it was eye-popping. (If anyone is curious, I suggest a little creative Web surfing—a lot of information is out there already.) As for clearing up this particular round of the continuing scandal, I believe that slowly the truth will come out and I will remain willing to cooperate in that process—even though it means that every newspaper report about the investigation seems to carry a photograph of me. By the time I had to testify, however, I was immune to it. Sure, some people may read a headline, glance at the pictures and thereafter associated me with the word "steroid." But anyone who bothers to read further would see that I wasn't the actual target of any investigation. And this latest round of revelations didn't change my position on the question of doping one iota. I can still sum it up in four words: I am against it.

Around the time I was called to testify, Dan, Charlie Wells, Tim and I sat down to discuss which meet to select for my comeback. It would have to be indoors because I couldn't wait for the outdoor season. At first, I wanted it to be a small one. Then I realized: *Who was I kidding?* Which small meet would attract sprinters of the caliber I needed in order to test myself? And at which small meet could I just blend in? In the end, since there'd be a media circus wherever I went, I decided to go for a meet in the U.S. At least I'd have some degree of comfort, as well as slightly less fuss—"athletics" being much bigger in Europe. We picked the Verizon Millrose Games, which took place in early February at Madison Square Garden in New York City— probably the most prestigious and historic (2004 would be its 96th year) indoor invitational meet in existence. If I couldn't be inconspicuous, I may as well go for broke.

When I got to New York I was nervous. I knew I'd win—I *never* doubt that—but I wanted to win resoundingly. I wanted to send a message: *I'm back!* The problem was not so much me being out of practice in racing—if anything, a crowd and the competition only motivate me further—it was running 60 meters. It's

NORMALLY, TRAINING WITH GUYS LIKE I DO, I'M FORCED TO GET MY ANGLES RIGHT BECAUSE ONLY THEN DO I HAVE A FIGHTING CHANCE TO STAY WITH THEM FOR A FEW METERS. **BUT IN JANUARY, THEY WERE LEAVING ME WAY BEHIND, JUST KILLING ME.** THAT NEVER HAPPENS.

I LOOKED UP INTO THE STANDS, PACKED WITH TRUE TRACK FANS, AND I SMILED TO MYSELF. "OH, IT'S GREAT TO BE BACK."

simply not my race. The 60m is all about the start, and my start was never my strong point. In the 100m I normally make my move and accelerate away from the pack around the 50- or 60-meter mark, which is obviously a useless tactic at this distance. But I had a new weapon in my arsenal. With Dan, I'd learned a new start, and it was what we concentrated on during my training in January.

By the time we reached the Caymans, I'd been in spikes for a couple of weeks. I was feeling great and running fine. But I was having a lot of problems with the new start. I was unable to prevent an enormous pause before my first step. When the gun went, instead of going straight forward, I was raising my head and shoulders first, popping up, going back down, and *then* starting to run. Normally, training with guys like I do, I'm forced to get my angles right because only then do I have a fighting chance to stay with them for a few meters. But in January, they were leaving me way behind, just killing me. That never happens.

It wasn't the prospect of the Millrose Games messing with my head, but rather the new start I'd learned from Dan not becoming automatic right away. The extension of my back leg, bringing my hips up higher in the blocks to convert my height into an advantage—it was logical and worked beautifully, but it was also new. My old crouching start would prove disastrous at Millrose, so there was no question of reverting to that, but I was still pausing after more than two weeks working on the new start. It was frustrating. But in the end, I aced it a little more than a week before we left.

The Millrose press conference at the storied New York Athletic Club was packed. As well as all the American reporters, I recognized a few who had made the trip over from Europe for my comeback. As expected, the first question was: "Are you nervous, Marion?" I'd debated with myself whether to admit to what I considered a sign of weakness in the past. I'd decided to tell the truth: "Yes!" I smiled. "I'm a little nervous." It felt good to say it. Rather than weakness, I thought, it was a sign I'm maturing, growing up a bit. In reality, my nerves were all about the distance being uncharted territory for me. I'd run the 60m only twice before, some five years ago, and I was never considered great for the first 30 meters, which was where these 60m specialists excelled. My opponents included Torri Edwards, Inger Miller (my old California rival) and Allyson Felix, a high school runner who had made a splash in 2003 by breaking my 200m high school record and was being touted as "the new Marion Jones." I doubted she was too happy about that, but in truth I saw myself in her. She had a lot of pressure on her at a young age, just like I had. But unlike my experience in high school, she had already signed a contract and was obliged to run. When I was her age, I was still running for fun, not for money, and I was loving it. I just hoped she was still able to enjoy it all and not be overwhelmed.

As far as the actual running went, *who* my competitors were didn't matter to me—I've never based my performance on comparison. My occasional attack of *What the heck was I thinking?* was all about the distance, plus some other variables. Normally I'm able to set the scene in my head for an upcoming race, but this time I couldn't picture it. It had been so long that I could barely visualize the other athletes. And running indoors was unfamiliar to me. Everything would be so close. I didn't know how I'd respond to that kind of chaos. It was a little scary. The day before the race, I had an up-close preview of my competitors during a final training session at the New York Armory—a facility I knew well from the vantage point of the announcers' box when I'd been asked to give the color commentary for races during 2003. Because the Armory is the premier indoor track in New York City, everyone who was competing in the Millrose 60m was training a few feet away from me. I barely registered them, though, because I was concentrating on what would be my best session of the year to date. My starts came off perfectly. Dan was pleased. I was ready.

The only time I had been inside Madison Square Garden before the 2004 Millrose Games was to attend a Knicks game, which resembled the scene at Millrose about as much as a basketball resembles a discus. The route to my backstage quarters went through a labyrinth of service elevators and shuttered snack concessions, through an empty theater and past storage rooms of cages full of yapping "athletes" for the next week's event: the Westminster Kennel Club Dog Show. When we finally reached it, my warm-up area was a dingy cordoned-off carpeted corridor on an upper level. It was kind of surreal and a blur. The evening came to life only when I was led, by an equally complicated route, to the track. The lights were intense and I was blinded for a second, but then the scene came into focus: the red track banked at the curves, the blocks set up at one edge of the straightaway ready for the short sprints, the jumping area and fat landing pad for the pole vault, athletes stretching in sweats on the carpet. I looked up into the stands, packed with true track fans, and I smiled to myself. *Oh, it's great to be back. It's great to be back among the people who really love our sport.*

My race was scheduled for 9:08 p.m. We'd planned my warm-ups accordingly, and I began to stretch and prepare around 8:30 p.m. I wasn't used to the cramped quarters; there was a whole assortment of athletes warming up on the back stretch of the track, everyone hyper-aware of the limited space, being careful not to run into each other—and the pole vault in progress only a few feet away. When it was clear that we wouldn't be starting on time, I sought out and found Allyson Felix to congratulate her on her '03 season. I asked how she was dealing with the pressure and how she was doing, and she seemed pleased to chat. It was great to finally put a face to the name—and if I could help her avoid encountering the unfriendliness I did when I started, that was a good thing.

By 10:15 p.m., Stacy Dragila was making her second attempt at a 15'6¼" Millrose pole-vault record and the "Fastest Kid in New York City" 50m dash still hadn't been run, and most of my nerves had gone home to sleep. But I was thoroughly enjoying the scene nonetheless. It felt incredible to rub elbows with the track world again, just to be in the warm-up area with all the athletes. I was also studying the starter at the same time, trying to get the pattern of how he was shooting the gun. I was determined to be vigilant in the starting blocks. I wouldn't relax too much for fear of having a brain fart—a *Huh? Where am I?* moment—but I didn't want to lock in too much either and risk a false start. The infamous "False Start Rule" had come into play since I had last competed. According to the new rule, if someone false-started, it could now be charged to the field, which meant that every athlete was held responsible. If there was a second false start, whether it was the same person who false started the first time or not, that athlete would be disqualified. There'd been an uproar over the rule change, but it stood nevertheless. At the Millrose, I figured, it just might work to my advantage: If everyone was wary of false-starting, then they'd most likely be a fraction slower off the mark. But I wasn't counting on that. Nor did I want to false-start myself.

By the time we lined up for the climactic women's 60m dash—at 10:20 p.m.—I figured that my study of the starter had paid off; I knew what to expect. Only I was wrong. All night the starter had been consistently prompt in pulling the trigger, but when our turn came he held us, and held us, and held us. I started to rock forward. When I didn't hear the pop, I started to rock back . . . and that's when he hit the gun. I was caught in exactly the position I was trying to avoid. Instead of having my hips up high and my fingertips barely grazing the track, I had my back knee bent with too much weight on my hands. Just like I'd been doing in the Caymans, I popped up, came back down and only then did I start to run.

A bad start.

▲ My start in the 60m dash at the 2004 Millrose Games in New York City was bad—exactly what I had been hoping to avoid.

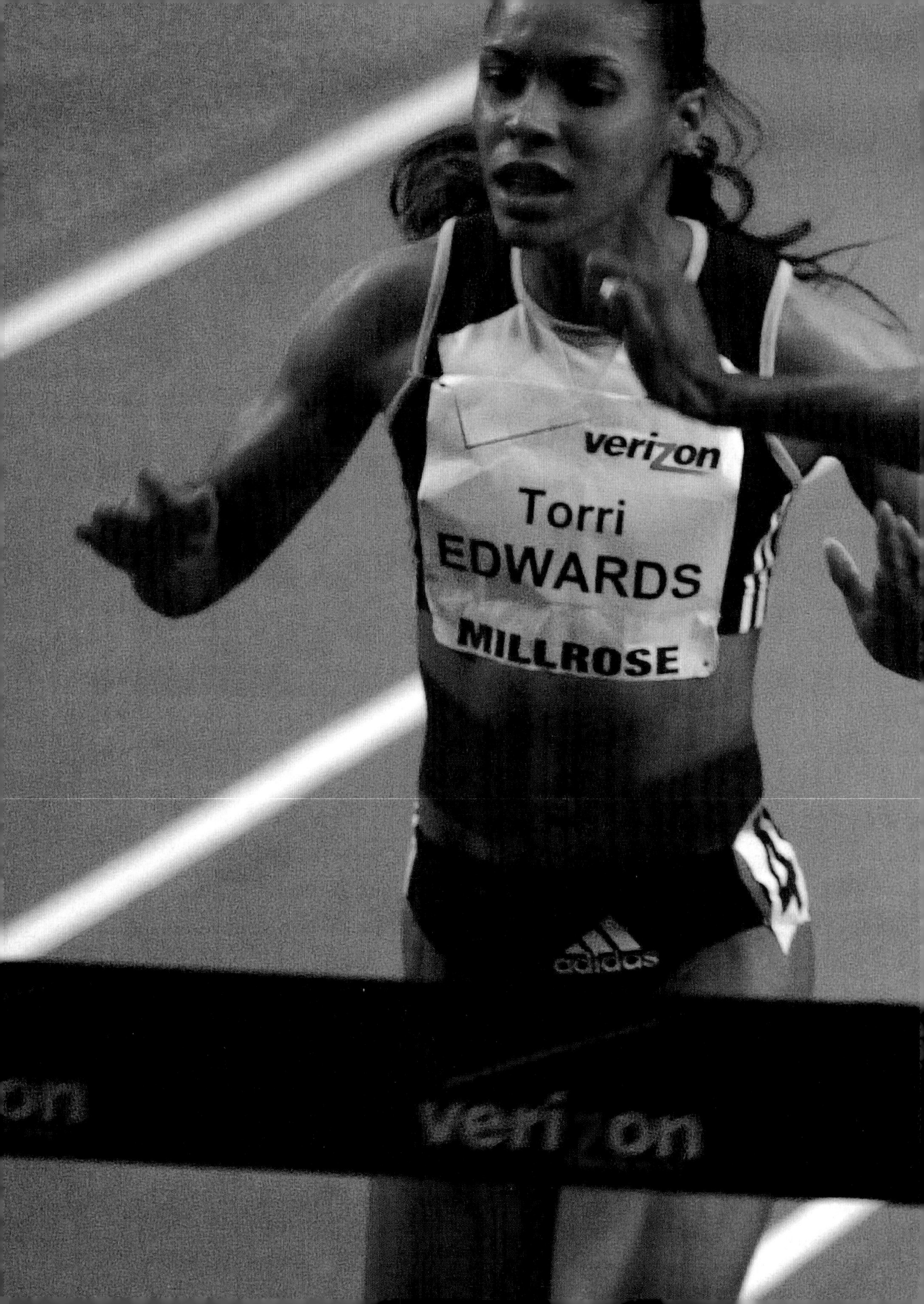
verizon
Torri
EDWARDS
MILLROSE
adidas
verizon

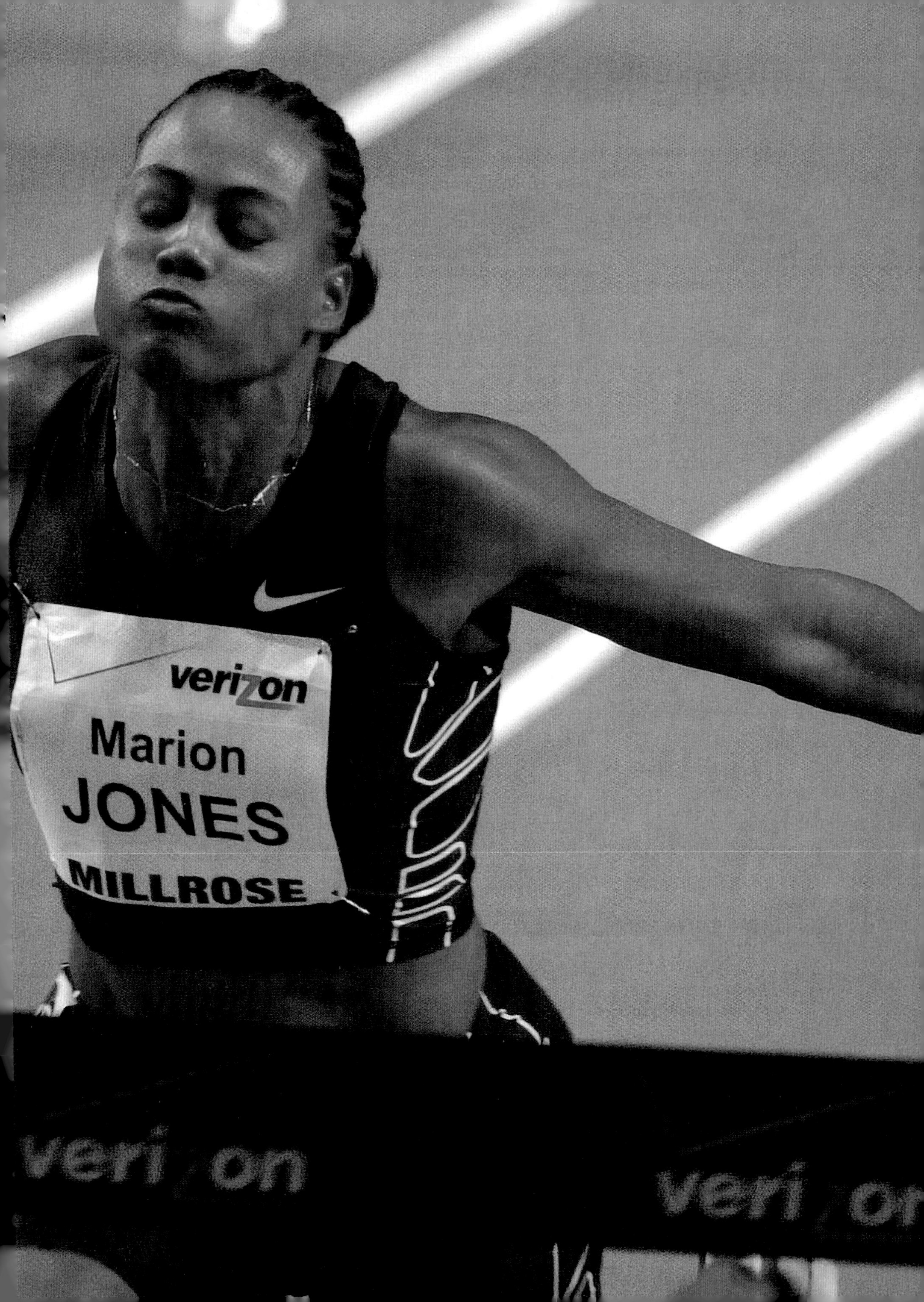
verizon
Marion
JONES
MILLROSE

I felt myself falling behind immediately. When I looked up, I saw the other runners a meter or so ahead of me. But I didn't panic. I didn't get tense. I simply found a higher gear and switched up to it. It felt fantastic. I was on a roll. I had so much momentum, if I'd had another 40 meters I'd have beaten them by miles. As it was, I just beat them. I ran through the tape and on through the tunnel under the stands. My time was 7.21.

The next day, we had an early-morning flight. I got home, took a 90-minute nap and went straight out to the track to train. I had so much left over from the race. The 60m had barely taken a toll. I felt fine. So what if my time hadn't been earth-shattering? I'd take the win, learn from it and move on to the next thing.

The next thing was a few weeks later: the Norwich Union Indoor Grand Prix in Birmingham, England. I entered the 60m again, but more important, I was going to make my long jump debut. And *debut* was the right word. It was my first chance to put my newly learned knowledge into practice. I would finally be jumping with the precision and skill I ought to have had all along. I had no more excuses, no more winging it on natural ability and a prayer. Three and a half years after my disappointing experience in Sydney, I was starting over.

Birmingham had typical English weather, drizzly and gray. It made staying in my hotel room all that much easier, but it also made the adrenaline coursing through my system hard to bear at times. I was ridiculously excited.

In the press conference two days before the event, I cornered the public address announcer, a gentleman I knew well from previous British meets: "Please, I need to ask you a favor," I whispered to him, "On Friday, can you not announce when I'm standing on the runway about to jump?" He laughed. In past meets, he'd always wait until just before I'd appear, then grab the mike: "Ladies and gentleman," he'd say. "Up on your feet. Make some noise. Marion Jones is about to jump. . . ." This time, I explained, I wanted to make my first jump in relative peace and quiet. I knew some people were bound to notice and start to clap, but it would take a while for the whole arena to catch on and by that time I'd have done it. I was afraid that the rhythmic, accelerating *clap-clap-clap* the crowd loves to do when a jumper is preparing would get me too hyped up. I didn't want to end up flying down the runway. I wanted to work on my *controlled* speed this time. I needed every ounce of concentration so that I wouldn't revert to my old, bad habits of sprint-fly-and-slam. The announcer said he'd try, but he didn't think it would be up to him.

I kept waking myself up the night before the competition. In my dreams, I was jumping repeatedly with my arms standing in for my legs. And every time I took off, I was thumping my hand on the headboard. Luckily, the hotel headboard was soft padded leather or I'd have been black and blue by morning. I wasn't surprised I slept fitfully, because I was delirious with excitement. I found out the day before that instead of the usual six jumps, we were getting only four, which put so much more pressure on each attempt. Normally, I take the first two jumps almost as warm-ups, to get into the swing of it, then I'd make sure the next two were legal and long enough to put me ahead. For the final two, I'd let it rip. I might easily foul, but I might also pull off something spectacular. That's when I'd really see what I could do. But now I'd have to be a bit more restrained. I'd have to make the first two look good and be legal, then win on what would normally be the middle ones, the safety jumps. On the positive side, I'd also discovered I had over an hour between the 60m and the start of the long jump, so I'd be able to relax for half an hour after the postrace press conference and get my head together for the big event.

◄ (previous page) Despite the bad start, I was
able to make up ground in the 60m at the
Millrose Games, eventually winning the race in
7.21 seconds.

▲ I posted a better time, 7.16 seconds,
in the 60m at the 2004 Norwich Union Grand
Prix in England than I did the week before at
the Millrose Games, but I came in second to
Kim Gevaert of Belgium.

The 60m was disappointing. The good news was that I ran a better time, 7.16, than at the Millrose. However, the Belgian sprinter Kim Gevaert's time was .03 seconds faster, and I had to settle for the silver medal. Of course I want to win every time I race, but I was philosophical about it. It was not my distance, and I was really there to jump. And jumping was next.

My friend the public address announcer didn't come through. He was right that it wasn't up to him—there was a commentator up in a booth and a camera earmarked just for me. The moment I took up position, the speakers crackled into action: "Okay, everybody! Marion Jones is on the runway! Let's hear it for Marion!" My first jump was horrible. And of course it was the only one for which I'd wanted to be relatively anonymous! After that, though they announced me every time, I'd settled into it and I didn't mind the crowd at all. Then, oddly enough, I got off the hook for my last jump because the entire crowd was looking the other way, cheering for an athlete who had just set a British record. In the end, it worked out perfectly. I was in control and on top of the world. Every one of my jumps was better and longer than the last. Even though I felt I was just starting to get it together when the competition was over, I still won. Not only that, but I was the only one of the six competitors not to foul on any of my jumps, and my winning 6.75-meter (22'1¾") jump was a whole 0.4 meters (15¼") longer than the best by the Spanish silver medalist, Concepción Montaner. I couldn't have been more pleased with that. It was a fitting end to my brief indoor season and a good start to my march toward a second Olympic Games.

As I write, it's spring 2004 and I'm gearing up for one of the great challenges of my life. All the outdoor competitions are preparation for one thing: Sacramento in July, the 2004 Olympic trials. I'm constantly being asked in which events I'll compete in Athens. I don't answer that question. Athens depends on Sacramento, and Sacramento is as far as I'm prepared to look at this point. Still, as you know by now, I am hoping to go for five again. But the relays are wild cards. This year, the 4x100m is especially up in the air. Inger Miller and Torri Edwards are each in a bit of a slump. Chryste Gaines and Kelli White are in trouble of a different sort, both of them having failed drug tests. So I really don't know who the coaches will line up with me. It will be interesting.

Chances are, you'll see a lot of me this spring and summer—and I don't mean just on the track. Before the Sydney Olympics a certain amount of attention was focused on me as a role model, an icon. It was fun and new to me at the time—and it was fairly shallow. Also, it was about image—not that it was necessarily a bad thing. On the contrary. Four years ago the sight of a powerful woman carried some shock value. Female muscles and strong opinions still bordered on transgressive in certain quarters back then. And the publicity suited who I was then, too—a young woman attempting an incredible feat. Now the world has moved on, and so have I. And so has my relationship to my image. The world is much more accustomed to female athletes now—thank goodness—so who I am has to have more of a story behind it. I take my duties and my impact as a role model seriously, which is partly why it's important for me to tell my story, my way. As I've matured and my life has become more complicated and also more rounded, so has the idea of me that's projected into the world. I don't want to be seen as some untouchable, unapproachable goddess (unbeatable, yes—always unbeatable). I want young girls—and women—to relate to me so they can identify with what I've achieved and apply it to their own lives.

Female athletes have always been respected less and paid less than our male counterparts. I think many male professional athletes take their responsibilities as public figures less seriously than we do because they take it for granted. Female athletes like me, and like my friends Mia Hamm and Lisa Leslie, work harder. We have to in order to be noticed at all. And instead of trying to steal each other's thunder, we work together because we share an outlook. We know how lucky we are compared to the female athlete of 30,

20, even 10, years ago. The road was paved by pioneering women like Althea Gibson, Billie Jean King, Kathrine Switzer, and Florence Griffith Joyner—and we're reaping the benefits. We don't usually have the big egos of the guys; we don't feel like we're taking money out of each other's pockets. Virtues and values like sharing, gratitude, humility and cooperation aren't necessarily seen as part and parcel of the professional athlete's life. But they could be. They should be.

Back in 2000, I didn't have to answer to or worry about anyone else. I did as I pleased. Now that's all changed. Like the majority of women in the world, I'm balancing many things in a full and sometimes chaotic life. A glossy portrait of me posed in a running outfit with an intense, determined look on my face is only one side of the picture. I want everyone to know that there's a regular, multifaceted woman behind the glamorous image. I want them to know that I love my family and I'd sacrifice anything for them. That I have a goofy side and a controlling side . . . and a weakness for ice cream. I don't think it's a separate, private issue that I detest shopping and spend most of my life in sweats. That finding a pair of jeans that fit snugly to my waist and my butt but also get over my big athlete's thighs is a real challenge. That when we're going out someplace elegant, I have seven outfits laid on the floor because I can't get it right. That the biggest joy of my life is when my baby son says "ma-ma-ma-ma"—even if he doesn't have a clue what it means. I want everyone to know that even if I'm in ads on TV and plastered on billboards 10 feet tall and interviewed by Oprah, I'm still a mom with a career. I may be in the fast lane, but I'm not larger than life.

# A GLOSSY PORTRAIT OF ME POSED IN A RUNNING OUTFIT WITH AN INTENSE DETERMINED LOOK ON MY FACE IS ONLY ONE SIDE OF THE PICTURE.

# COMPETITIONS: A HISTORY

**1997**

| | |
|---|---|
| April 19, 1997 | Barnett Bank Invitational, Gainesville, Florida – Long Jump – 1st place – 21'8" |
| April 26, 1997 | University of Pennsylvania Relays, Philadelphia, Pennsylvania – Long Jump – 1st place – 21'6" |
| May 24, 1997 | Gatorade Invitational, Knoxville, Tennessee – 100m – 1st place – 11.09 |
| June 12, 1997 | USA Track & Field Championships, Indianapolis, Indiana – 100m – 1st place – 10.97 |
| June 15, 1997 | USA Track & Field Championships, Indianapolis, Indiana – Long Jump – 1st place– 22'9" |
| July 2, 1997 | Athletissima, Lausanne, Switzerland – 100m – 2nd place – 10.90 |
| July 4, 1997 | Bislett Games, Oslo, Norway – 100m – 1st place – 11.06 |
| July 7, 1997 | DN Galan, Stockholm, Sweden – 200m – 1st place – 22.16 |
| August 3, 1997 | IAAF World Championships in Athletics, Athens, Greece – 100m – 1st place – 10.83 |
| August 9, 1997 | IAAF World Championships in Athletics, Athens, Greece – Long Jump – 10th place – 21'9" |
| August 9, 1997 | IAAF World Championships in Athletics, Athens, Greece – 4x100m – 1st place – 41.47 – Chryste Gaines, Gail Deevers and Inger Miller |
| August 13, 1997 | Weltklasse, Zurich, Switzerland – 100m – 2nd place – 10.97 |
| August 13, 1997 | Weltklasse, Zurich, Switzerland – 200m – 1st place – 21.76 |
| August 16, 1997 | Herculis, Monte Carlo, Monaco – 200m – 1st place – 21.92 |
| August 22, 1997 | Memorial Van Damme, Brussels, Belgium – 100m – 1st place – 10.76 |
| August 24, 1997 | Grand Prix, Cologne, Germany – 200m – 1st place – 21.93 |
| August 26, 1997 | ISATF, Berlin, Germany – 100m – 1st place – 10.81 |
| September 6, 1997 | Toto, Tokyo, Japan – 100m – 2nd place – 10.91 |
| September 13, 1997 | IAAF Grand Prix Final, Fukuoka, Japan – 200m – 1st place – 21.84 |

**1998**

| | |
|---|---|
| February 25, 1998 | Melbourne Track Classic, Melbourne, Australia – 100m – 1st place – 11.01 |
| February 28, 1998 | IAAF Outdoor Meet, Sydney, Australia – 200m – 1st place – 21.98 |
| March 7, 1998 | Gunma International Indoor, Maebashi, Japan – 60m – 1st place – 6.95 |
| April 19, 1998 | Mount San Antonio College Relays, Walnut, California – 400m – 1st place – 50.11 |
| April 25, 1998 | University of Pennsylvania Relays, Philadelphia, Pennsylvania – 4x100m – DQ – 42.75 – Passion Richardson, Inger Miller and Gail Deevers |
| April 25, 1998 | University of Pennsylvania Relays, Philadelphia, Pennsylvania – 4x200m – 1st place – 1:29.64 – Tameka Roberts, Inger Miller and Nicole Green |
| May 3, 1998 | Shizuoka Grand Prix, Shizuoka, Japan – 200m – 1st place – 22.56 |
| May 5, 1998 | Mito Invitational, Mito, Japan – Long Jump – 1st place – 23'1¾" |
| May 9, 1998 | IAAF Japan Grand Prix, Osaka, Japan – 100m – 1st place – 10.79 |
| May 12, 1998 | World's Fastest Woman Competition, Chengdu, China – 100m – 1st place – 10.71 |
| May 31, 1998 | Prefontaine Classic, Eugene, Oregon – 100m – 1st place – 10.77 |
| May 31, 1998 | Prefontaine Classic, Eugene, Oregon – Long Jump – 1st place – 23'11¾" |
| June 7, 1998 | Meeting Città di Padova, Padua, Italy – 200m – 1st place – 21.94 |
| June 14, 1998 | Grand Prix, Helsinki, Finland – 100m – 1st place – 10.86 |
| June 19, 1998 | USA Track & Field Championships, New Orleans, Louisiana – 100m – 1st place – 10.72 |
| June 20, 1998 | USA Track & Field Championships, New Orleans, Louisiana – Long Jump – 1st place – 23'8" |
| June 21, 1998 | USA Track & Field Championships, New Orleans, Louisiana – 200m – 1st place – 22.24 |
| July 5, 1998 | Gugl-Meeting, Linz, Austria – 100m – 1st place – 10.84 |
| July 9, 1998 | Bislett Games, Oslo, Norway – 100m – 1st place – 10.82 |
| July 14, 1998 | Golden Gala, Rome, Italy – 100m – 1st place – 10.75 |
| July 14, 1998 | Golden Gala, Rome, Italy – Long Jump – 1st place – 23'8¾" |
| July 20, 1998 | Goodwill Games, New York City, New York – 200m – 1st place – 21.80 |
| July 29, 1998 | Gaz de France Paris Saint-Denis, Paris Saint-Denis, France – 100m – 1st place – 10.88 |
| July 29, 1998 | Gaz de France Paris Saint-Denis, Paris Saint-Denis, France – Long Jump – 1st place – 22'10½" |

**1998**

| August 3, 1998 | Mai, Malmo, Sweden – 100m – 1st place – 10.87 |
| August 8, 1998 | Herculis, Monte Carlo, Monaco – 100m – 1st place – 10.72 |
| August 12, 1998 | Weltklasse, Zurich, Switzerland – 100m – 1st place – 10.77 |
| August 12, 1998 | Weltklasse, Zurich, Switzerland - Long Jump – 1st place – 23'11¾" |
| August 25, 1998 | Athletissima, Lausanne, Switzerland – 100m – 1st place – 10.72 |
| August 28, 1998 | Memorial Van Damme, Brussels, Belgium – 100m – 1st place – 10.80 |
| September 1, 1998 | ISATF, Berlin, Germany – 100m – 1st place – 10.81 |
| September 5, 1998 | Grand Prix Final, Moscow, Russia – 100m – 1st place – 10.83 |
| September 11, 1998 | IAAF World Cup in Athletics, Johannesburg, South Africa – 200m – 1st place – 21.62 |
| September 12, 1998 | IAAF World Cup in Athletics, Johannesburg, South Africa – 100m – 1st place – 10.65 |
| September 13, 1998 | IAAF World Cup in Athletics, Johannesburg, South Africa – Long Jump – 2nd place – 22'11¾" |

**1999**

| March 19, 1999 | All Africa Invitational, Roodeport, South Africa – 200m – 1st place – 21.84 |
| April 22, 1999 | Mount San Antonio College Relays, Walnut, California – 400m – 1st place – 50.79 |
| April 24, 1999 | University of Pennsylvania Relays, Philadelphia, Pennsylvania – 4x100m – 2nd place – 43.42 – Susanthinka Jayasinghe, Tameka Roberts and Inger Miller |
| April 24, 1999 | University of Pennsylvania Relays, Philadelphia, Pennsylvania – 4x200m – 1st place – 01:30.02 – Susanthinka Jayasinghe, Inger Miller and Faliat Ogunkoya |
| May 30, 1999 | Prefontaine Classic, Eugene, Oregon – 200m – 1st place – 21.81 |
| June 10, 1999 | Grand Prix, Helsinki, Finland – 200m – 1st place – 21.91 |
| June 12, 1999 | Grand Prix Invitational, Raleigh, North Carolina – Long Jump – 2nd place – 23'0" |
| June 24, 1999 | USA Track & Field Championships, Eugene, Oregon – Long Jump – 2nd place – 22'0⅗" |
| June 27, 1999 | USA Track & Field Championships, Eugene Oregon – 200m – 1st place – 22.10 |
| June 30, 1999 | Bislett Games, Oslo, Norway – 200m – 1st place – 22.22 |
| July 2, 1999 | Athletissima, Lausanne, Switzerland – 100m – 1st place – 10.80 |
| July 7, 1999 | Golden Gala, Rome, Italy – 200m – 1st place – 22.19 |
| July 21, 1999 | Gaz de France Paris Saint-Denis, Paris Saint-Denis, France – 200m – 1st place – 22.99 |
| July 26, 1999 | Gugl-Meeting, Linz, Austria – Long Jump – 2nd Place – 22'2⅗" |
| July 30, 1999 | DN Galan, Stockholm, Sweden – 200m – 1st place – 22.07 |
| August 7, 1999 | Norwich Union British Grand Prix, London, England – 100m – 1st place – 10.80 |
| August 11, 1999 | Weltklasse, Zurich, Switzerland – 200m – 1st place – 22.11 |
| August 14, 1999 | Herculis, Monte Carlo, Monaco – 200m – 1st place – 22.15 |
| August 22, 1999 | IAAF World Championships in Athletics, Seville, Spain – 100m – 1st place – 10.70 |
| August 27, 1999 | IAAF World Championships in Athletics, Seville, Spain – 200m – Marion injured during semifinal race and did not compete for the rest of the season. |

**2000**

| April 16, 2000 | Mount San Antonio College Relays, Walnut, California – 400m – 1st place – 49.59 |
| April 29, 2000 | University of Pennsylvania Relays, Philadelphia, Pennsylvania – 4x100m – 1st place – 42.33 – Chryste Gaines, Torri Edwards and Inger Miller |
| April 29, 2000 | University of Pennsylvania Relays, Philadelphia, Pennsylvania – 4x200m – 1st place – 01:27.46 – LaTasha Jenkins, LaTasha Colander-Richardson and Nanceen Perry |
| May 13, 2000 | IAAF Japan Grand Prix, Osaka, Japan – 100m – 1st place – 10.84 |
| May 13, 2000 | IAAF Japan Grand Prix, Osaka, Japan – Long Jump – 4th place – 20'6¾" |
| June 17, 2000 | Grand Prix Invitational, Raleigh, North Carolina – Long Jump – 2nd place – 21'6" |
| June 24, 2000 | Prefontaine Classic, Eugene, Oregon – 100m – 1st place – 10.93 |
| June 24, 2000 | Prefontaine Classic, Eugene, Oregon – Long Jump – 1st place – 22'10¾" |

## 2000

| | |
|---|---|
| June 30, 2000 | Golden Gala, Rome, Italy – Long Jump – 1st place – 22'¼" |
| June 30, 2000 | Golden Gala, Rome, Italy – 100m – 1st place – 10.91 |
| July 15, 2000 | Final Olympic Trials, Sacramento, California – 100m – 1st place – 10.88 |
| July 16, 2000 | Final Olympic Trials, Sacramento, California – Long Jump – 1st place – 23'½" |
| July 23, 2000 | Final Olympic Trials, Sacramento, California – 200m – 1st place – 21.94 |
| August 1, 2000 | DN Galan, Stockholm, Sweden – 100m – 1st place – 10.68 |
| August 5, 2000 | Norwich Union British Grand Prix, London, England – 100m – 1st place – 10.78 |
| August 11, 2000 | Weltklasse, Zurich, Switzerland – Long Jump – 1st place – 22'9" |
| August 11, 2000 | Weltklasse, Zurich, Switzerland – 100m – 1st place – 10.95 |
| August 25, 2000 | Memorial Van Damme, Brussels, Belgium – 100m – 1st place – 10.83 |
| September 1, 2000 | ISATF, Berlin, Germany – 100m – 1st place – 10.78 |
| September 23, 2000 | Olympic Games, Sydney, Australia – 100m – 1st place – 10.75 |
| September 28, 2000 | Olympic Games, Sydney, Australia – 200m – 1st place – 21.84 |
| September 29, 2000 | Olympic Games, Sydney, Australia – Long Jump – 3rd place – 22'8½" |
| September 30, 2000 | Olympic Games, Sydney, Australia – 4x100m – 3rd place – 42.20 – Chryste Gaines, Torri Edwards and Nanceen Perry |
| September 30, 2000 | Olympic Games, Sydney, Australia – 4x400m – 1st place – 3:22.62 – Jearl Miles-Clark, Monique Hennagan and LaTasha Colander-Richardson |
| October 5, 2000 | Grand Prix Final, Doha, Qatar – 100m – 1st place – 11.00 |

## 2001

| | |
|---|---|
| April 28, 2001 | University of Pennsylvania Relays, Philadelphia, Pennsylvania – 4x400m – 1st place – 03:23.4 – Monique Hennagan, Michelle Collins and LaTasha Colander-Richardson |
| May 12, 2001 | Princeton Invitational, Princeton, New Jersey – 100m – 1st place – 11.12 |
| May 27, 2001 | Prefontaine Classic, Eugene, Oregon – 200m – 1st place – 22.26 |
| June 9, 2001 | U.S. Open, Palo Alto, California – 200m – 1st place – 22.70 |
| June 24, 2001 | USA Track & Field Championships, Eugene, Oregon – 200m – 1st place – 22.52 |
| June 29, 2001 | Golden Gala, Rome, Italy – 100m –1st place – 10.96 |
| July 4, 2001 | Athletissima, Lausanne, Switzerland – 100m –1st place – 11.04 |
| July 6, 2001 | Gaz de France Paris Saint-Denis, Paris Saint-Denis, France – 100m – 1st place – 10.84 |
| July 9, 2001 | Nikaia, Nice, France – 100m – 1st place – 11.25 |
| July 13, 2001 | Bislett Games, Oslo, Norway – 100m – 1st place – 10.94 |
| July 22, 2001 | Norwich Union British Grand Prix, London, England – 100m – 1st place – 11.00 |
| August 6, 2001 | IAAF World Championships in Athletics, Edmonton, Canada – 100m – 2nd place – 10.85 – Marion's first loss in 2001 |
| August 10, 2001 | IAAF World Championships in Athletics, Edmonton, Canada – 200m – 1st place – 22.39 |
| August 11, 2001 | IAAF World Championships in Athletics, Edmonton, Canada – 4x100m –2nd place – 41.71 – Kelli White, Chryste Gaines and Inger Miller |
| August 17, 2001 | Weltklasse, Zurich, Switzerland – 100m – 1st place – 10.94 |
| August 24, 2001 | Memorial Van Damme, Brussels, Belgium – 100m – 1st place – 10.86 |
| September 4, 2001 | Goodwill Games, Brisbane, Australia – 100m – 1st place – 10.84 |

## 2002

| | |
|---|---|
| April 21, 2002 | Mount San Antonio College Relays, Walnut, California – 400m – 1st place – 50.46 |
| April 27, 2002 | University of Pennsylvania Relays, Philadelphia, Pennsylvania – 4x400m – 1st place – 03:23.41 – Michelle Collins, Jearl Miles-Clark, LaTasha Colander-Richardson |
| May 26, 2002 | Prefontaine Classic, Eugene, Oregon – 100m – 1st place – 10.90 |
| June 8, 2002 | U.S. Open, Palo Alto, California – 100m – 1st place – 11.20 |

| | |
|---|---|
| **June 12, 2002** | Golden Spike, Ostrava, Czech Republic – 200m – 1st place – 22.32 |
| **June 22, 2002** | USA Track & Field Championships, Palo Alto, California – 100m – 1st place – 11.01 |
| **June 23, 2002** | USA Track & Field Championships, Palo Alto, California – 200m – 1st place – 22.35 |
| **June 28, 2002** | Bislett Games, Oslo, Norway – 100m – 1st place – 10.96 |
| **July 2, 2002** | Athletissima, Lausanne, Switzerland – 100m – 1st place – 11.04 |
| **July 5, 2002** | Gaz de France Paris Saint-Denis, Paris Saint-Denis, France – 100m – 1st place – 10.89 |
| **July 12, 2002** | Golden Gala, Rome, Italy – 100m – 1st place – 10.89 |
| **July 19, 2002** | Herculis, Monte Carlo, Monaco – 100m – 1st place – 10.84 |
| **August 16, 2002** | Weltklasse, Zurich, Switzerland – 100m – 1st place – 10.88 |
| **August 23, 2002** | Norwich Union British Grand Prix, London, England – 100m – 1st place – 10.97 |
| **August 30, 2002** | Memorial Van Damme, Brussels, Belgium – 200m – 1st place – 22.11 |
| **August 30, 2002** | Memorial Van Damme, Brussels, Belgium – 100m – 1st place – 10.88 |
| **September 6, 2002** | ISATF, Berlin, Germany – 100m – 1st place – 11.01 |
| **September 14, 2002** | Grand Prix Final, Paris, France – 100m – 1st place – 10.88 – Tim Montgomery breaks the Men's 100m World Record! |
| **September 20, 2002** | IAAF World Cup in Athletics, Madrid, Spain – 100m – 1st place – 10.90 |
| **September 20, 2002** | IAAF World Cup in Athletics, Madrid, Spain – 4x100m – 2nd place – 42.05 –Chryste Gaines, Inger Miller and Gail Deevers |

| | |
|---|---|
| | Marion does not compete during the 2003 track and field season because she is pregnant. |
| **June 28, 2003** | Timothy Lois Montgomery is born at 9:58 p.m. |

| | |
|---|---|
| **February 3, 2004** | Verizon Millrose Games, New York City, New York – 60m – 1st place – 7.21 |
| **February 20, 2004** | Norwich Union Indoor Grand Prix, Birmingham, England – Long Jump – 1st place – 22'1⅞" |
| **February 20, 2004** | Norwich Union Indoor Grand Prix, Birmingham, England – 60m – 2nd place – 7.16 |
| **April 18, 2004** | Mount San Antonio College Relays, Walnut, California – 200m – 4th place – 23.02 |

# PHOTOGRAPHY

**Marion Jones thanks:** Mom, thank you for being my everything. Albert, thank you for teaching me to play and love sports and for letting me tag along for so long. IRA, thank you for being my silent supporter. To coaches Jarvis, Sims, Walker, Brown, Green, and Mason, thank you for teaching, guiding, exposing, and putting up with me. Eddie, thank you for sacrificing an entire year away from your wife. Marjorie, thank you for being Monty's Nana and always being there for us. Kate, thank you for finding the words and putting them together and making this feel so easy. Tim, thank you for making me laugh and enjoy life and sharing true love with me. And lastly, for my beloved Monty, thank you for waking up every morning with a smile. Thank you for the pure joy you bring into all of our lives. This book is dedicated to all of you who have shaped my life and continure to do so.

**Kate Sekules thanks:** first and foremost, Marion. You've made writing your book a total pleasure. Never was a goddess less of a diva. Thanks to the team at Melcher: to Charlie Melcher and Duncan Bock; to Lindsey Stanberry for taking care of a million details; and especially to John Meils, for managaing to make editing fun. Thanks also to Sarah Chalfant, wonder agent, and to Scott, for everything.

**Melcher Media thanks:** Marion Jones, for being so open and forthcoming about her life and for sharing her time. Many thanks to Joe Pollard, Adam Roth, Rory Rubin, Tim Phelan and everyone behind the scenes at Nike; to Charlie Wells, Rich Nichols, and Kim Gerraty; to Larry Kirshbaum and Dan Ambrosio at Warner Books; to David Brown, Julia Joern, Lauren Nathan, Lia Ronnen, Shoshana Thaler and Megan Worman at Melcher Media; and to Max Dickstein, Sajan Kuriakos, Elizabeth Johnson, Steve Mallin, Janie Matthews, Matthew Septimus and John Shostrom.